ENEMIES OF GOD

Timothy E. Pace

PAGE PUBLISHING, INC.
Conneaut Lake, PA

First originally published by Page Publishing 2021

ISBN 978-1-6624-6221-4 (pbk)
ISBN 978-1-6624-6222-1 (digital)

Printed in the United States of America

To several exceptional people who have helped and mentored me in my walk with Christ. Many have gone on to be with the Lord, and some are still giving me good advice and godly counsel. To these, I owe a debt that cannot be repaid: Mr. and Mrs. Jim Graham; Col. and Mrs. John E. Tabor; Pastor and Mrs. Dan Hellmintoler; Pastor and Mrs. Derrick Youngblood; Pastor and Mrs. Gene W. Amason; Mr. and Mrs. Billy Bush who has been a great mentor over the years; Mr. and Mrs. L. T. Nowell and family; and Mr. and Mrs. Jim Perry.

Last but not least, I could not do anything without the support of my loving wife, Sharron. Without her, I would not function as I should. She has been in continuous support both in the good times as well as in the bad. She is part of God's favor over my life, and I am overwhelmed by her love and dedication for the Lord and for me.

PART 1

Enemies of God

James 4:4 NKJV states, "Adulterers and adulteresses! Do you not know that friendship with the world is enmity with God? Whoever therefore wants to be a friend of the world makes himself an enemy of God."

James, the half brother of Jesus, wastes no time alerting the early Christians who were being persecuted for following Jesus about the dangers of being friends with the world. He was encouraging them to be diligent in keeping themselves free of any ungodly influences of the pagan culture of their time. This same warning can be applied to the church today. Given the current state of apostasy in the western church, we, too, are close to becoming the enemies of God. We are slowly and quietly drifting away from God in our worship and teaching throughout the church.

The postmodern church frequently uses the same attractional model as the corporate world. In other words, we are using carnal means to attract carnal men. We are appealing to their senses rather than to their hearts. In doing so, we will be required to maintain those fleshly standards to keep them. The truth is that if we are not careful, we will find ourselves at odds with God as well.

Association with the wrong crowd will eventually affect your lifestyle (see 1 John 2:15). Those who love the world and the things it offers don't love God. Likewise, those who love God don't love the world or the things the world offers. The love for God and the love for this world are incompatible. The word *world* in this verse is not speaking about the planet we call earth. It is referring to the world system. Satan, by deception, has control over the world system and blinds the minds of men who refuse to follow God.

However, if we will be diligent and contend for the faith, we can avoid finding ourselves on the wrong side of the Lord God. Vance Havner, a minister whom Billy Graham described as the most quoted minister of our time, explains it another way:

> [1]How many nice, comfortable, lovely people rest smilingly in church pews, their conscience drugged, their wills paralyzed, in self-satisfied stupor, utterly unconscious of their danger while the Lord of the Lampstands warns them, "I am about to spit you out of My mouth."

The enemies of God defined

Let's look further by asking the question, Who are the enemies of God, and what makes them as such? By simple definition, an enemy loathes or hates another and seeks to harm, contradict, and fight the one he is set against. Thus, an enemy of God opposes His divine purposes as well as His presence in this world. The Bible repeatedly shows that the enemy of God is a self-centered, carnal person seeking the world's pleasures over that which pleases God. By nature, he is arguing with the Creator. Until repentance comes, he will remain in a dangerous predicament with God. The Apostle Paul stood as an enemy to God before his conversion, as he persecuted the early Christians. He was determined to perform what he considered to be a religious obligation and duty. Still, his actions were against the will of God.

All through Israel's history, those who opposed God were counted as His enemies. Even though the Israelites were appointed by God to be special people, they continued to rebel against Him. The results of their persistent rebellion brought the judgment of God to His people. His standards have not changed!

> How often they provoked Him in the wilderness,
> And grieved Him in the desert! (Psalm 78:40 NKJV)

In all their affliction He was afflicted, And the
Angel of His Presence saved them; In His love
and in His pity He redeemed them; And He bore
them and carried them All the days of old. But
they rebelled and grieved His Holy Spirit; So He
turned Himself against them as an enemy, And
He fought against them. (Isaiah 63:9–10 NKJV)

Do you not know that to whom you present yourselves slaves to obey, you are that one's
slaves whom you obey, whether of sin leading to
death, or of obedience leading to righteousness?
(Romans 6:16 NKJV)

There will always be consequences for sin, whether you are a
believer or not. But as believers, we cannot afford the indulgence of
sin because it allows Satan access to our lives. Sin enables the devil
to produce death in our lives, so the only way to stop it is to repent
and ask God for forgiveness, which He will certainly give. This allows
God to remove the sin, thereby removing Satan and his strongholds.

When people consistently rebel against God, He eventually
gives them over to a reprobate or debased mind. In short, God will
enforce their decision to live as they please; sin no longer convicts
them because their conscience has been seared as with a hot iron (see
1 Timothy 4:2; Romans 1:28). This is the mind that has no restraints.
There is no longer any conviction of sin. Those who are reprobate
know they are wrong but no longer care. This also describes the state
of a person who has "passed the point of no return" with God. As
Romans 1:8 explains, God has revealed Himself to every person who
has ever walked the earth so no one will have any excuse before the
Father. God is long-suffering and patient, but He is not forever suf-
fering. And there is a limit to His willingness to deal with a man (see
Genesis 6:3). *After a period of time, individuals who continually reject
Him are hopelessly headed for hell because people cannot come to the
Father except when the Spirit draws them.*

Sign of the times

Paul predicted that as the final days approached, the Lord would send a strong delusion to those who ignore the truth of God's Word (see 2 Thessalonians 2:11). This describes a time when people will deliberately reject the truth of God's Word, thus becoming the enemies of God. Those who fall under this delusion are more than simply ignorant concerning what the Bible teaches. Paul, in fact, was speaking about the ones who are very much aware of the truth but reject it with intent. Whenever one deliberately rejects the truth of God's Word, they are, in a very real sense, choosing to be at odds with God by their own free will. The question we must ask is, if a person leaves the truth of God's Word, then to whom or to what do they turn? The scriptures provide us an obvious answer. They are choosing to follow the devil and his lies. And while it is not God's will that any should perish, He will always enforce your decision to reject the only hope of salvation available.

First Timothy 4:1 NKJV states, "Now the Spirit expressly says that in latter times some will depart from the faith, giving heed to deceiving spirits and doctrines of demons."

Enemies are deceived

In Matthew 24, we read where the disciples asked Jesus about the end-times. In describing the signs concerning the end, He said, "Take heed that no man deceive you" (see also 2 Peter 2:1–2; Jude 3–4). Why the warning about deception? Because the human heart has an almost inexhaustible capacity for being deceived. For the most part, the cause of this deception is based on our own selfishness. Satan, in the beginning, was selfish and self-serving. He was and still remains filled with pride. This self-serving characteristic has been passed down to mankind because Adam chose to disobey what God had commanded. So it is only natural that we want what we want when we want it, even if our desires go against God. We often fail to acknowledge the sin in our lives because acknowledging it requires us to change.

First John 2:16 NKJV states, "For all that is in the world—the lust of the flesh, the lust of the eyes, and the pride of life—is not of the Father but is of the world."

The Hebrew word for *deception* comes in many forms. Still, the core implication is that someone has been "lured" or "enticed" to believe something obviously false. So where does deception begin? As in the garden, deception often starts outside of yourself. It may come to you in one fatal dose, but most often, it comes in unassuming small quantities while being hidden with a partial truth. The only actual test of its authenticity is to compare what you are hearing to the Word of God. Intelligence, reasoning, nor logic can protect you from deception, but God's Word can always be trusted.

In Genesis 3:13, we see how Eve was deceived when Satan presented a lie as the truth. He had to use deception because he had no power to force anything upon her or Adam. The only thing he could do was to try to get them to destroy themselves. To do this, Satan had to plant a thought in her head that was contrary to God's Word to overcome her. The devil knows that if he can get us to consider things contrary to God's Word, doubt and unbelief can eventually lead us to sin. Sin is conceived through our thoughts and established through meditation (see Hebrews 11:15). The best way to stop the birth of sin is to prevent its conception (see James 1:15). The secret to winning against Satan many times is simply thinking as we should. If we are grounded in the Word of God, then we will most likely recognize the deception when it comes.

Not much has changed in our day when it comes to deception. A person becomes the enemy of God by turning from God's truth to the lies and deception of Satan. This is done willingly with having prior knowledge and understanding of the Word. They will close the eyes of their understanding and harden their hearts so that they cannot see or understand. They decisively and actively live a lie and think that their good works can cleanse them from sin. Those who think this way have never been more deceived. It's more than just being ignorant of the Word of God but a deliberate effort to rebel.

Jeremiah 11:10 NKJV states, "They have turned back to the iniquities of their forefathers who refused to hear My words, and they have gone after other gods to serve them; the house of Israel and the house of Judah have broken My covenant which I made with their fathers."

Again, notice Jesus's warning to His disciples about deception in Matthew 24. He warned them of deception because choosing to follow the Lord for a season does not mean that you can't fall away by choice (see John 3:18). Judas was just as much a part of Jesus's ministry as the other eleven. He healed the sick and raised the dead just like the others, but he decided to go after what the world offered, which cost him in the end. On the other hand, Peter was used in the same manner as Judas and was even guilty of denying Christ, but he repented and thus was saved. Jesus never turns people away, nor does He force anyone to stay, but neither will He compromise His standards in order to keep them.

The God we serve is long-suffering and willing to spare His enemy for a season. He is not in any hurry to avenge Himself. In fact, it is His mercy and compassion that stays the wrath off the sinner, giving them every chance to repent. God is patient, kind, and forbearing. While the Lord is patient and kind, He will not always strive with man (see Genesis 6:3). This is why it's essential to seek the Lord while He may be found and call upon Him while He is near (see Isaiah 55:6; John 6:44). So anyone who desires God is doing so under the leadership of the Holy Spirit. Therefore, if the Holy Spirit ever stops urging a person towards repentance, they cannot be saved.

Reprobate mind

When a person consistently rejects the Lord, they are given over to a reprobate mind after a certain amount of time. The phrase *reprobate mind* is found in Romans 1:28 and explains how God has abandoned those who rebel against Him as godless and wicked people. The reprobate is the one whom God has rejected and who has (see Hosea 4:6) been left to their own devices. This describes perfectly the enemy of God who "suppress the truth by their wickedness," and it is upon these people that the wrath of God rests (see Romans 1:18). The Greek word translated "reprobate" in the New Testament

10

is *adokimos*, which means literally "unapproved, that is, rejected; by implication, worthless [literally or morally]."

Further still, a reprobate mind has a working knowledge of God and is familiar with His commandments. However, they have very little desire to please God. The one with a reprobate mind will always live a corrupt and selfish life. Sin will always be justified and acceptable to them and is considered as normal behavior. Having been rejected by God, they are forever damned because they cannot come to the Lord without the Holy Spirit's influence.

Consider for a moment the consequences of those actions. Paul spoke of those whose minds and consciences are defiled (see Titus 1:6). They are disqualified from entering heaven. There is no hope for them in the eternal heavenly realm. If people would simply stop and consider the cost of rejecting Christ, maybe they would reconsider what God has offered. For some, Jesus only adds a new intellectual dimension to their life. They will often compare themselves to others who are in the same condition. Sadly, they are all headed for eternal hell.

Delusion

> The coming of the lawless one is according to the working of Satan, with all power, signs, and lying wonders, and with all unrighteous deception among those who perish, because they did not receive the love of the truth, that they might be saved. And for this reason God will send them strong delusion, that they should believe the lie, that they all may be condemned who did not believe the truth but had pleasure in unrighteousness. (2 Thessalonians 2:9–12 NKJV)

What is delusion, and how does it come? The word *delusion* means "wandering, the absence of a goal, mental straying, wrong opinion, error in morals or religion." Those who experience this delusion will have chosen to walk off the right path of truth into ways

11

of the world, which results from believing the devil's doctrines. The word *delusion* can also be described as a deliberate false belief that one consciously chooses as a life of spiritual fantasy. The deception is received as being reality despite knowing the truth. Delusion is much like deception but has a much stronger meaning. Deception simply means that a person has been misled about something through false information, leading to misbelief, but not in every instance. Delusion moves past deception. The deliberate acceptance of the lie develops into a belief system despite being contradicted by reality. Sadly, today's post-modern generation seems deluded because they reject God's Word deliberately and intentionally.

In Romans 1:21–32, Paul gave several descriptive and progressive steps that leads one away from the true revelation of God. The first step is not to glorify Him as the supreme, all-knowing, and unquestionable God. Adam and Eve questioned God's intent behind His command not to eat of the tree of the knowledge of good and evil (Genesis 3:1–6). Because Satan had planted the seed of doubt in their minds, they began to question God's purpose for their lives. His attack led them to think that there was something more for them. Therefore, when we doubt Him, we actually exalt "self" and become rebels.

Secondly, an enemy is not thankful. Adam and Eve lacked nothing before they rebelled. Everything was provided for their well-being. They had no need for anything because they were content with what they had until Satan convinced them to question God's provision for their lives. Therefore, today, the enemy of God cannot be satisfied. They are always looking for something other than God's will. Thankfulness for what the Lord has given is a sign of humility and will help keep "self" in its proper place. Paul tells us that we should be thankful and content with whatever we have.

After these first two steps have been taken, then the individual's mind is free to begin imagining foolish, wicked, and idolatrous thoughts. This leads to a hardened heart (see Mark 6:52) and a reprobate mind (see Romans 1:28). The Lord, being full of grace and compassion, would never give people a strong delusion that would keep them from receiving salvation. The Lord is "not willing that any perish, but that all should come to repentance" (see 2 Peter 3:9). So how do we understand this verse? When people reject the truth of God, they are, passing judgement upon themselves by their choice. He is just enforcing their own decisions. This only happens to those who don't love the truth. If men persist in rebellion, then God gives them over to their own ways, which will damn their souls. Those who reject God are simply operating the law of sowing and reaping.

Narrow-minded

Christians are often defined by several unpleasant characteristics and labeled with many names, and, to our shame, some are deserved. But the one attribute that is feared by most is that of being narrow-minded. It is associated with being dogmatic, religious, ignorant, and not willing to listen to or tolerate other people's views. Everyone desires to be accepted among their peers and thought of as being in touch with the day's culture, yet being narrow-minded about the kingdom of God is this very mindset that Jesus celebrated. Of all the words Jesus could have used to describe how we should think and live our lives, He chose *narrow*. The enemy of God is anything but narrow-minded.

Matthew 7:13–14 NKJV states, "Enter by the narrow gate; for wide is the gate and broad is the way that leads to destruction, and there are many who go in by it. Because narrow is the gate and difficult is how it leads to life, and few find it."

The enemy of God chooses to walk the "broad way." He decides to live this way because he has no fear of the Lord and has set himself up as the ruler of his life. Tragically, people today tend to view God's kingdom as a democracy ruled by the majority's wishes. The current teaching that there are many roads to the Father is deceptive and dangerous because it offers only what it needs to provide for the needs of the individual and is based on emotion and personal preference. But the King says there is only one path to the Father. The kingdom of heaven is His and not ours. He reigns sovereignly and has the final say about who enters and by what means. Not all roads lead to heaven. One direction goes to eternal bliss, while as others go to eternal damnation.

Heaven's gate is restrictive but not because of poor construction or that the way is poorly marked. We must also remember that it is not our kingdom but God's. The Almighty is under no obligation to anybody, nor does He allow any entry other than by the methods He chooses. Jesus publicly pointed out that He alone was God's provision for the forgiveness of sins and entrance into eternal life. There is no other way! The gate is narrow because unholy men can only approach a holy God through the shed blood of Jesus Christ (1 Timothy 2:5–6; Hebrews 9:11). This goes against anything the enemy of God believes. But the truth is that it has to be God's way or no way at all. There are no other options given.

Furthermore, men enter into the kingdom one at a time, as one might go through a turn-style or enter the subway. We are never saved in groups but as individuals. Salvation occurs when people realize that they are incapable of saving themselves and call upon God's mercies. When we come to Christ, it's as if we are coming to meet Him much like when Nicodemus met with Jesus. It will be the most personal encounter with God. It will be more than just giving up certain sins and vices. It will be a heart change given by God alone that will enable us to live for Him. This is not something that can be done outside of God's sovereign will through the Holy Spirit. But the enemy of God will think that he can save himself when the time comes.

Changing perception

There was an article written some time ago about faith in *The Times* London, saying, [2]"Faith in the Nation: Religion, Identity, and the Public Realm in Britain Today, the archbishop argued that the Church of England deserves its place as the established church of Great Britain because it now serves as a 'public utility' serving the common good." Dr. John Sentamu, the archbishop of York, said, "The Church of England should be open for use by people of any religion or none, like a hospital." Given that sort of thinking, it's no great wonder that the body of Christ seems to be slowly fading away with today's cancel culture. Given the lack of moral direction and the overabundance of society's choice, it's not hard to understand why our choices often lead to failure.

Is the church in America now being perceived as a public utility? Have we lost the purpose of our existence? I certainly believe in the church that Christ established. She has been given all things that pertain to this life and to godliness. The same power of God that works through Jesus rests within our spirit that provides us with the ability to raise the dead, heal the sick, and cast out demons. We are to be transformed into His likeness and do the same works as He did on the earth. Our mandate from Jesus is to lead the lost to Him and teach them how to be a disciple rather than just how to be a good church member. But the church I see now is not the one I read about in the Bible. The church as a whole no longer experiences the miracles as the early church did. And if they do appear, they are quickly discounted as fake. It seems that we have lost our prophetic voice and are no longer relative to the "enlightened" culture of today's society.

For way too long, the body of Christ has sat back and remained silent concerning the spirit of compromise that plagues our society and the church. We are trying to be all things to all men by being neutral to the same crowd. We basically permit sin's existence by not saying anything, thereby giving it permission to quietly grow in our own hearts. We, by our silence, can quietly become the enemies of God ourselves. Could it be that we are fellowshipping at the very tables Jesus would have overturned? Maybe we have become like the people whom the Prophet Amos has described. Amos 6:1 NKJV states, "Woe to you who are at ease in Zion, And trust in Mount Samaria, Notable persons in the chief nation, To whom the house of Israel comes!"

Jesus had much to say to the church in Laodicea.

> Because you say, "I am rich, have become wealthy, and have need of nothing"—and do not know that you are wretched, miserable, poor, blind, and naked—I counsel you to buy from

Me gold refined in the fire, that you may be rich; and white garments, that you may be clothed, that the shame of your nakedness may not be revealed; and anoint your eyes with eye salve, that you may see. As many as I love, I rebuke and chasten. Therefore, be zealous and repent. (Revelation 3:17–19 NKJV)

This sounds a lot like the modern-day church found in America. We have plenty of money and material possessions, which has led many to believe are self-sufficient. We certainly have perfected a great attractional model of church. But Jesus has a far different opinion of what the church really ought to be.

As a whole, the church holds very little moral bearing on our society. We have allowed just enough of the world's influence into the church that we are beginning to sound very much like the ones we are trying to win. Could it be that the church, like Peter, is now warming herself at the fires of the enemy? We must take care not to be warming ourselves at the fire of unbelievers because it will always lead us into temptation (see James 1:8). Some say that Christians must be the agents of change in our society. I agree that we are to reach the lost, but not at the expense of holiness. Do the means always justify the end? No matter how we should relate to today's culture, the sanctuary of Sunday-morning church shouldn't resemble Saturday night's concert hall. There must be a difference.

As usual, the religious machinery continues to grind, and the gears continue to mesh. The image given in the scriptures concerning the churches in Revelation is powerful in one sense yet paints a picture of profound disgust in the eyes of the Lord. The point being made by Jesus is that unless the church repents, it could be utterly rejected as well. While we may have an excellent reputation, we may be close to becoming the enemies of God. When our reputation is more outstanding than our true character, we are doing it wrong. Cultural character is a value measured in the marketplace of the world. Godly character is the value found in the sight of God. In choosing to look and act like the world, we may allow the spirit of the world to gain a foothold. Shall we continue to serve two masters?

Revelation 3:1 NKJV states, "And to the angel of the church in Sardis write, 'These things says He who has the seven Spirits of God and the seven stars: I know your works, that you have a name that you are alive, but you are dead.'"

As born-again believers striving to function in a sinful world, we should remember that this world is not our home. Our home is in heaven, and we are subjects of the King of Glory (see Philippians 3:20). Paul warned us about minding earthly things and encouraged us to be heavenly-minded. To be carnally minded is certain death (see Romans 8:6). When we develop the mentality that we are citizens of heaven rather than earth, our actions will influence others for Christ. They can see the reality of our relationship with Jesus simply by living our lives as the Word tells us. The scriptures are clear about how the Lord regards the believer's friendship with the world. He considers it adultery. It's fraternizing with the enemy. Those who cross the lines to fellowship with God's enemy will eventually find themselves at odds with God.

Our nation is floundering

Not only has our nation drifted from the principles of God but also is making a determined effort to forget Him altogether. In all fairness, this indictment cannot be levied against every church in America. Thankfully, many ministries continue to follow Christ and lead the lost to Jesus. However, as a nation, we have forgotten the blessings that God has bestowed on us. We no longer can say that we are a Christian nation but rather only a nation with Christians living in it.

There was a time when Christianity was accepted in our nation. Then as our country began to prosper, we drifted into a post-Christian culture that merely tolerates Christianity. Now our culture is totally anti-Christian, attacking every belief and value of our faith. The poet Mantuanus expresses this thought well: "Ye who desire to live a godly life, depart; for, although all things are lawful at Rome, yet to be godly is unlawful."

Public prayer is no longer allowed. The teaching of basic godly morals is forbidden in most institutions of higher learning. The right to worship as one sees fit is coming under more scrutiny than ever before, even making congregational singing a crime in some states. Some churches have been closed because they failed to follow specific government mandates. The nation still claims to trust in God, but we continually lean on our own understanding. We have turned a blind eye to government officials' immoral acts, whose lies, deceptions, and hypocrisy have made us the laughingstock of the world, yet we still refuse to repent of our sin.

No longer do we approach God in fear and trembling as a nation. We now worship gods of our own design and ask God to join us. We regularly call evil *good* and good *evil*. We shun the light and celebrate the darkness without shame by calling it entertainment. What a terrible thing, but how accurately this describes the day we live in. Today it is offensive to the majority, to tell the truth and have godly moral values. Those without biblical morals are called good, and those with Godly standards are called bigots, racists, and at best, out of touch with today's society. Evil is now good, and good is now evil among the policy makers of our day. God help us!

This nation alone has routinely murdered over a million unborn babies each year, and our government has declared it to be legal. The results of such debauchery is that the blood of the innocent now stain our collective hands as a nation. It doesn't matter how many courts uphold abortion to be legal; it is still the murder of innocent human beings. There is a penalty for those who offend the little ones (see Matthew 18:6). How can God bless what He hates? According to the Word of God, we are standing as enemies to the Creator.

Psalm 7:11–12 NKJV states, "God is a just judge, And God is angry with the wicked every day. If he does not turn back, He will sharpen His sword; He bends His bow and makes it ready."

Our pulpits have allowed wolves in sheep's clothing to preach a watered-down gospel by omitting repentance, the work of the cross, and becoming a sold-out disciple for Christ. They no longer preach about the blood of Christ being shed for our sins because it is offensive to the sinner. We have failed the Great Commission miserably by upgrading the gospel to be socially relevant and more acceptable. The enemy of God is very much at home under these conditions and has no plans to change.

God has been ejected from our schools, and murder and chaos have taken His place. Our children are being brainwashed by liberal and progressive teachers who teach against the principles of godly morals. We are producing homeless minds so now our kids are killing other children. The sons and daughters are killing their parents, and the parents are killing their children without any remorse. In addition, it is now compulsory that we accept the sexually perverted lifestyles of others as being normal when such acts are an abomination unto God. And still, we call ourselves a Christian nation. How can God bless what He has condemned? I say we are becoming the enemies of God!

Second Peter 2:22 NKJV states, "But it has happened to them according to the true proverb: 'A dog returns to his own vomit,' and, 'a sow, having washed, to her wallowing in the mire.'"

Another gospel

The Galatians had drifted away from the gospel Paul had proclaimed clearly to them (see Galatians 1:6–9). Today the average churchgoer believes that belief is the same thing as faith. However sincere they may be, they are on the road to hell. There has to be more to salvation than just belief. The scriptures show that even the devil believes, so believing alone is not enough for salvation.

James 2:19 NKJV states, "You believe that there is one God. You do well. Even the demons believe—and tremble!"

We can read in Matthew 23:15 that Jesus took note of the evangelistic methods of the scribes and Pharisees. These Pharisees, who were the children of hell, were making others twice the sons of hell. They were very religious, yet they wrongly represented God and stood as the enemies of God. They were not truly following the Lord but rather following their own traditions. Likewise, many today appear passionate about God. They attend church and might even serve in some leadership role. Still, if their real motives were revealed, they would be just like this group that Jesus was rebuking.

An entire generation has been sold the lie that all you have to do is raise your hand to be saved rather than have a broken and contrite heart. It is essential for a person to know why we should accept Christ and become a disciple. Yes, we should teach about the mercy and love of God. No one can debate that He has poured His love out for anyone who will repent and come to Him. But it is more than that! The whole counsel of God is required. The sinner must realize the desperate situation they are in. They have to know in their heart that they must change and embrace that change. Salvation is about fully committing ourselves to the lordship of Jesus. If we are to win the lost to Christ, shouldn't we use the same early apostles' methods? Do we need to update the gospel to accommodate those who feel intimidated by the truth? The gospel is not our inviting Christ into our lives but rather our accepting His invitation to join Him.

Isaiah 5:20–21 NKJV states, "Woe to those who call evil good, and good evil; Who put darkness for light, and light for darkness; Who put bitter for sweet, and sweet for bitter! Woe to those who are wise in their own eyes, And prudent in their own sight!"

Reprobate minds

Reprobate people are those who have been abandoned by God because of their decisions and are without hope of salvation. Think of that for a moment! How horrible it will be to be totally forsaken by the only one who could save them from a burning hell. I believe that the sinner who arrives in hell will realize that they didn't have to be where they are. Their predicament is of their own doing, and there is no recourse given. This could also apply to Christians who have renounced their faith in Christ (see 2 Corinthians 13:5–7; 2 Timothy 3:8; Titus 1:16; Acts 5:5), thus becoming the enemy of God.

For the unsaved, there lurks a quiet danger. John 6:44 tells us, "No man can come to me, except the Father which hath sent me draw him." Without the drawing power of the Holy Spirit, no man can be saved.

Romans 1:28 NKJV states, "And even as they did not like to retain God in their knowledge, God gave them over to a debased mind, to do those things which are not fitting."

You cannot obtain salvation without surrendering to the lordship of Jesus Christ. In today's evangelism method, the call to come to Jesus is given politely without the demand for submission as a disciple. To refuse Jesus as Lord while accepting Him as Savior will never produce salvation. [3]A. W. Pink was quoted saying, "Salvation is by grace, by grace alone. Nevertheless, divine grace is not exercised at the expense of holiness. It never compromises with sin." In other words, without repentance, there is no lordship, nor is there any salvation.

Paul gets to the reason of our predicament here, saying, "Once you were alienated from God and were enemies in your minds because of your evil behavior" (see Colossians 1:21). Notice the terms *in your mind*. You are not separated from God only by your evil works any more than you are saved by your good works. This alienation comes from within and takes hold of a person's very being. This is why people find reconciliation with God so problematic. Their minds are set toward the ways of the sinful world; thus, the whole man is set against his Creator as an enemy. Mankind is, by birth, separated from God because of the great fall of Adam. It is a state of sinfulness that comes with everyone born on the earth. However, this alienation and hostility between God and man begins in our mind as well as our spirit. It is not God who rejects us, but rather, it is us who rejects God. We reject God by wanting to go our own way, living our own lives, and being our own god.

Consequently, since it is our minds that lead us away from God, it will require the renewing of our minds to restore us back to God. What we think is vital in forming who we are. Proverbs 23:7 NKJV states, "For as he thinks in his heart, so is he. 'Eat and drink!' he says to you, But his heart is not with you." A person will not operate differently from what is in their heart. The scriptures tell us that it is vitally important to guard our hearts because it is the center of control for our lives. We can deceive ourselves into thinking that we are without sin, but our actions will eventually reveal what is really in us.

That's why we are told to renew the mind and not be conformed to the world (see Romans 12:2). It is through the operation of the mind that one can understand that a savior is needed. Paul's prayer was that "the eyes of your understanding being enlightened; that you may know what the hope of His calling is, what are the riches of the glory of His inheritance in the saints" (Ephesians 1:18 NKJV). The phrase *eyes of your understanding* is a comparison referring to the ability to observe with the mind. We have to have our minds opened by the Holy Spirit to perceive spiritual truth (see Luke 24:45) by assimilating God's Word into our hearts.

The unregenerated spirit living from a carnal mind can never be subject to God. And by its very nature, it will always, without exception, follow after the flesh's desires. A few individuals may quietly acknowledge God's existence. But for the most part, the Almighty remains immaterial to anything concerning their life, and they consider God as being nonessential. In their view, the Creator is now serving at some cosmic help desk only to be called upon in times of need. As society begins to minimize God as part of their daily lives, rituals, and worship, He becomes practically nonexistent.

Some of the more religious people in our society may have a form of godliness but are powerless against the works of darkness in truth. They have no standing with God and are trying to live in two different worlds, which is impossible to do. This is what the Bible calls being double-minded. You can't live in two different worlds. Jesus said, "You can't worship two gods at once. Loving one god, you'll end up hating the other." You must choose one or the other. Love of one generates contempt for the other. You can't worship both God and the world. A double-minded man is one whose devotion is divided between God and the world system. His attention is divided, and as a consequence, he is unstable and unable to receive from God.

The enemy of God will most often desire a savior from the penalty of their sin but not from the power of sin over their lives. They will live according to the world's principles and deny the fact that God has set either heaven or hell as their inevitable end. Death is not the end of our existence but rather the beginning of our final destination. We must always keep in mind that everyone will spend eternity somewhere. It will be with the Lord in heaven or in hell as an enemy of God.

The enemy of God has deliberately made a choice to rebel against God. It is a choice that each of us must make for ourselves. Either we become disciples of Christ or disciples of the world. Sadly, many professing Christians never practice the teachings of Christ. They may have emotionally agreed to specific facts about Jesus and joined a church, but they are not saved. They often can quote Bible verses, believing that it is enough to be religious, but if their heart does not change, they were never saved. If there is no conviction of sin, no repentance, and no commitment to Christ's lordship, then they are not saved by any measure and stand as an enemy of God.

The Apostle Paul warned the church to "stay away" from those who choose to follow after the world and its offerings (see 2 Timothy 3:5). Indeed, we must be willing to extend grace to our fellow believers and the unsaved so as not to present a legalistic attitude. Still, there must be a dividing line between what is acceptable and what cannot be allowed into the body of Christ. The example given in Acts 19:8–9 shows Paul separated the disciples from those who denied the power of the gospel. There were several times Paul told his followers to withdraw from ungodly people who were the enemies of God (see Romans 16:17; 1 Corinthians 5:11; 2 Thessalonians 3:6; 1 Timothy 6:5). This is the same warning that James was issuing.

Secular thinking leads the way

Essentially defined, secularism says that man does not need God or anything connected to Him. It is a philosophy whose primary objective is abolishing all religious elements from society. Secularism, also known as secular humanism, promotes the thought that there are no objective or absolute truths that distinguish between moral and immoral behavior. It is nonspiritual thinking that shifts man's focus from God to nature, reason, and science. The core belief is that the only things that really matter are those that have to do with this world, with no belief in an afterlife. By and large, truth is subjective to the individual's ideas, and that truth exists along the pathway of choice. Our children are being taught this philosophy and it is having a negative impact on the nation. Our nation becomes more like ancient Israel where "everyone did what was right in his own eyes" (see Judges 17:6, 21:25). When God's ways are removed from society, we can be sure that the pathway for the demise of that society is set.

This is the mindset for the enemy of God. They will continue their lives as if God were not around to see their actions. Therefore, life's emphasis is to enjoy everything that the world offers, not considering the coming judgment. Moses found himself in the same situation of having to choose between the Egyptian world and God. Having been reared in the palaces of Pharaoh, he knew the taste of luxury and wealth. Thankfully Moses decided to follow after the Lord's plan for his life. Sin, if we choose to follow it, does provide temporal pleasure to our senses, but that pleasure has a short life span and a very high price.

Hebrews 11:24–26 NKJV states, "By faith Moses, when he became of age, refused to be called the son of Pharaoh's daughter, choosing rather to suffer affliction with the people of God than to enjoy the passing pleasures of sin, esteeming the reproach of Christ greater riches than the treasures in Egypt; for he looked to the reward."

As a philosophy, secularism pursues to understand life based on the carnal principles of the world. It deals with facts only and gives no room for spiritual thought. Secularization, which is a much more dangerous process, is when God and religion are pushed to the faraway margins of life. So far, that faith makes no significant contribution to the policies and life values adopted by society. The secularization process is often much more subtle, quietly becoming more dangerous to the Christian because it looks like everyday life. Christians are often deceived before they are even aware of its effects, chiefly because we have assimilated to the day's culture. Christian beliefs that were once considered reasonable and acceptable are now regarded as awkward, embarrassing, or even dangerous. Today's believer struggles with the secular challenge by adopting the standards of the world with our thoughts and speech as a new way of life. We are becoming more and more at home in spiritual Babylon, forgetting that this world is not our home.

This thinking has produced a generation of spiritual vagabonds with no anchor point and no real bearing in life. They have been told that it is entirely reasonable to have many opinions and ideas about what defines morally correct behavior. Now that the church is becoming more conformed to secular beliefs and cultural practices, traditional religion no longer makes sense, nor is it attractive. Those values taught in our forefathers' church are seen as old-fashioned and out of touch with today's current trends. As the church allows worldly thinking to distort and adjust the reference line of morality, we not only enter into the camp of the enemy but also will enable him to come into ours. We make sure everyone feels at home in our home camp when, in reality, the enemy has made us feel more at home in his.

When God's enemy is confronted with the gospel of holiness, they are offended. It often makes them come to a place of decision about their lives and how they are living. Sin is brought to the forefront, and a choice has to be made. This, in turn, causes a more trimmed-down secularized version of Jesus to be offered. It is made to look more accepting and inviting to avoid offending their secular sensibilities, which has no Jesus at all.

Many times, services are conducted in such a way as to avoid the feeling of being "in church." We want to make people feel comfortable. Still, Jesus never made the religious world comfortable about their sinful lifestyle. Can it be that, as a church, we have become so much like the world that the sinner feels no conviction for the heart's actual condition? While it is essential to use different methods and resources to reach the lost, there must be caution in how the gospel is presented.

Believers in Jesus Christ are simply in the world and not of it, nor part of its values (see John 17:14–15). We are totally different species than those who are not saved. That is not to say that we are different in terms of our physical nature but rather in our spirits. Second Corinthians 5:17 NKJV states, "Therefore, if anyone is in Christ, he is a new creation; old things have passed away; behold, all things have become new." True believers still can sin, but when they do, they will not like it. They can't stay there and be comfortable because they have received a new heart.

As believers, we are citizens of a different world. We should have no desire to live as we once did because our natures have been changed; instead, we must conform ourselves and our minds to that of Jesus Christ (see Romans 12:1–2). This is a daily activity and commitment. Holiness is not being better than someone else. Author Jerry Bridges, in his book [4] *The Pursuit of Holiness*, offers this definition:[3]

> To be holy is to be morally blameless. It is to be separated from sin and, therefore, consecrated to God. The word signifies separation to God and the conduct befitting those so separated... To live a holy life, then, is to live a life in conformity to the moral precepts of the Bible and in contrast to the sinful ways of the world.

One can be morally correct and still have no connection with Christ. Take Judas for example. He lived and ministered with Jesus just as the other disciples, but his heart was different. In fact, he was trusted enough to be the treasurer of the group. He was treated as a brother, yet his heart brought the kiss of death to Jesus. His actions and words had been so sure, his pretense so perfected, that none of them suspected that he would betray the Lord. In the end, Judas was possessed by Satan and was damned for all eternity. How deceptive can appearances be! How wicked can a person's heart become!

> Therefore put to death your members which are on the earth: fornication, uncleanness, passion, evil desire, and covetousness, which is idolatry. Because of these things the wrath of God is coming upon the sons of disobedience, in which you yourselves once walked when you lived in them. But now you yourselves are to put off all these: anger, wrath, malice, blasphemy, filthy language

out of your mouth. Do not lie to one another, since you have put off the old man with his deeds, and have put on the new man who is renewed in knowledge according to the image of Him who created him. (Colossians 3:5–10 NKJV)

We can't deny the fact that being in the world yet abstaining from it is difficult. The pull and influence of an ungodly society can be unrelenting and, at times, most attractive. The scripture commands us to be separated from the world system as well as those who adhere to the world's practices. There is tension here because Jesus also said that we are the salt and light of the earth (see Matthew 5:13–14). So if we are to be light to those in spiritual darkness, we must be different from those without light. How can we expect the lost and dying world to come to Jesus if we walk in spiritual darkness ourselves?

Separated in our beliefs

As Christians, we are to live separated from the world and all its ungodly influence. This can be a difficult task to be sure but one that is required of the Lord. The enemies of God always have their own systems of opinions and beliefs. They think and act according to the flesh and not according to the Word of God. You can be sure that the carnal man will cater to the desires of the flesh. But as believers, we are to practice what the Bible teaches both day and night (see Joshua 1:8). We must guard against falling into the foolish sayings, beliefs, and practices of a sinful and godless world. How can we, as believers, save someone from drowning if we are going under as well? It all comes down to how we think! We cannot consistently live our lives differently than what we believe in our hearts. And if we want to change our actions, we have to change our thinking first. Anything less is just an attempt at behavior modification, not actual heart change.

Additionally, Christians should have little dealings with those who openly live sinful lives other than ministering the gospel to them and we should always treat them with kindness and love. Paul made it very clear by his comparisons that being unequally yoked with unbelievers just won't work. Believers and unbelievers live different lives and are not anything alike. We should be compared as the light to the darkness. We, as Christians, have a different set of rules that govern our lives. According to the Bible, any Christian who doesn't see this conflict is deceived and must closely examine their own lives. As believers, we do not have the right to condemn because we ourselves are saved only through God's mercy. The Bible commands us to be blameless as believers, not rendering evil for evil but preaching the gospel in love and truth.

Still, we must abstain from even the appearance of evil. It appears that evil associations may have corrupted good manners for Paul to write about it (see 1 Corinthians 15:33). Paul was appealing to the Corinthians to separate from the fellowship that was hindering them. If we are ministering the Word of God, then we have to associate with those who don't think like us. But we must limit the level of our participation to the gospel only. We can see a much greater application of this truth throughout the Scriptures. When we associate with evildoers without regard to our own hearts, we tend to follow the crowd. Some would disagree with this, thinking that if one is strong spiritually, then association with evil can't hurt. Paul said we are deceived if we believe that.

> Do not be unequally yoked together with unbelievers. For what fellowship has righteousness with lawlessness? And what communion has light with darkness? And what accord has Christ with Belial? Or what part has a believer with an unbeliever? (2 Corinthians 6:14–15 NKJV)

We also have to be careful to live our lives as born-again Christians and not as religious Pharisees. Jesus has given us something that the lost world desperately needs, and that being hope and freedom from the power of sin over their lives! If we don't live our lives in the way Christ has commanded, then others will see us as just another religious group. Our lives should reflect Jesus so much that those outside the faith notice something "different" about us. Christians who live, think, and act contrary to Christ do Him a great disservice. We can't expect people to come to Jesus if we live according to the standards found in the world. The millennials say, "We don't believe what you are saying because we can see how you act." People are not looking for a better Christianity or a new and improved church. What they desire is a real relationship with God. They want an authentic experience with Jesus that changes their lives.

Jesus was separated from the world system but was still able to reach people. Jesus was separated unto God so that He might reach us. Likewise, we should separate ourselves unto the Lord so that we might see others come to Jesus as we did. It is not our holiness that causes people to seek after Him because the Holy Spirit is the only one who can do that. But if people cannot see Jesus in us, it may be because we are so connected with this life's affairs that we are just like them (see Mark 4:19).

> They are not of the world, just as I am not of the world. Sanctify them by Your truth. Your word is truth. As You sent Me into the world, I also have sent them into the world. And for their sakes I sanctify Myself, that they also may be sanctified by the truth. (John 17:16–19 NKJV)

To be effective, we need to be careful to maintain the proper balance (see John 17:11–12). We should avoid any connecting relationships where we are more influenced by others' negatives than Jesus's positives. Believers and unbelievers are as different as light and darkness or someone who has faith and those with no faith (see 1 Corinthians 15:33). When confronted with God's enemies, we should witness to them, but that doesn't mean we have to join with them.

Second Corinthians 6:17–18 NKJV states, "Therefore 'Come out from among them And be separate,' says the Lord. 'Do not touch what is unclean, And I will receive you. I will be a Father to you, And you shall be My sons and daughters,' Says the LORD Almighty."

Being in the world means we can enjoy the stunning creation God has given us. But our devotion belongs to Him. Moreover, we are to be prosperous and be a blessing to those around us who are less fortunate. Again, we must take care not to immerse ourselves in the world's moral values, nor are we to chase after worldly pleasures leading to sin. We will either serve Jesus or the world, and there's no other option. It's the cost of being His disciple.

Luke 9:62 NKJV states, "But Jesus said to him, 'No one, having put his hand to the plow, and looking back, is fit for the kingdom of God.'"

The believer must develop a proper biblical worldview, so we can overcome the world's influence by seeing the beauty in Christ. A biblical worldview sees the world through absolute and objective moral truths found in the Bible. For example, we accept that Jesus came to give His life a ransom for many (see Matthew 20:28). Everything about what Christ offers us has eternal value to it. Nothing is lost with Christ but that which hinders us from seeing Him. C. S. Lewis once said, [5]"Whatever is not eternal is eternally out of date."

The western church has tried so hard to be relevant to the culture just to draw people to the church. But have we really impacted our society for Christ, or have we hindered the kingdom? The question begs, Who has changed who? Have we intermingled so well with the culture that we have become unnoticed and immaterial to society? The church should be welcoming to all, but it must remain different from the world. Our services should be a time of worship with a sense of holiness. There must be a difference in the way we approach His throne! There must be a sense of God's presence in the atmosphere. The presence of God cannot be engineered with all the effects of a rock concert. Anything less than His presence is simply a work of our flesh.

Can Christianity truly compete with the world? It is a difficult task for sure because the world seems to have more to offer. The world says, "Come on in, the water's fine," while the church says, "Abstain from even the appearance of evil." The world system offers pleasures, while the church provides a cross. Today's society gives us the freedom to live as we wish while Jesus teaches total commitment to Him as a bond servant. Make no mistake. We should strive for excellence in ministry and do what we can to reach people, but how far and at what cost do we proceed? Do the means always justify the end? The good news is that we are not supposed to compete against anyone. We, indeed, need to do everything for the glory of the Lord. But our motivation for providing quality ministry should not be to compete with the world. [6]A. W. Tozer warned, "Worship is no longer worship when it reflects the culture around us more than the Christ within us."

We need evidence of power

When we read that the Holy Spirit came upon the early believers, we can see that they actually had the power to do great things for God. But now we can scarcely see anything out of the ordinary happening in the church. It has been said of some churches that if the Holy Spirit didn't show up in the service, there would be no noticeable difference. If we do not see the gifts in operation or do not see people commit their lives to Christ, can we assume that the Holy Spirit is not present?

We seem to be afraid of the power of the Holy Spirit. Maybe we are hesitant to allow Him access to our lives because it's bound to change us. While some may argue that no man has the right to judge another, that no man can determine if anyone is saved. I would counter that with the statement that no one who has ever really experienced God has come away unmarked. True salvation will always bear some fruit. We must certainly always extend grace to those who are young in the Lord. But after a season, there should be some growth. This is not to say that their lives are perfect, but they live more by the spirit of God than their flesh (see Romans 7:18).

The characteristic of an enemy of God is that they desire a savior but not a lord. You cannot have it both ways. Some would like forgiveness of sin but nothing of holiness. Accordingly, if there is no change in your life actions, then there has been no heart change. Why should those outside the faith come to Christ if they see no proof of what Christianity says it has? Their accusations of hypocrisy, to some degree, are, in fact, accurate if very little difference can be seen between the two worlds. Why can't they claim to be saved, to know Jesus, and live a life of sin just as other so-called Christians do? That is what they see in many who are claiming to know Christ. Undaunted by the truth, they remain optimistic; however, that God's great love for humanity will hold off His willingness to bring judgment against their sin. They only believe what has been shown to them. Sadly, to our indictment, they fail to realize that man's opinion has no value in the courts of God.

Falling short

The most significant mistake for the person living at odds with God is to think that they can save themselves by their self-made righteousness or by doing good deeds. They don't consider the fact that they will fall well short of God's standard of holiness even by their best efforts (see Romans 3:23). People are so impoverished in their sin that they cannot possibly save themselves. They deny or ignore the fact that they must have a savior. No other religion provides a savior. To some degree or another, the world's other religions teach that the burden of salvation is upon people's own shoulders. Christianity thankfully has a Savior, and His name is Jesus; God Himself provided salvation for mankind. When we accept any other method other than trusting in Jesus and His righteousness, we will become an enemy. God's righteousness is the standard by which all men will be judged, and we will all miss the mark without Jesus.

The enemies of God often deny their dangerous predicament. They have not realized, as Jonathan Edwards once preached, [7]"that they are hanging over the fires of an eternal hell only by a single strand of God's mercy." They fail to recognize that it is only by God's mercy that they are allowed to live another moment in time. People don't go to hell as payment for their sinful lifestyle. They go there because they reject the Giver of Life by a simple decision not to confess Jesus as Lord and Savior. They are living as rebels against God. It is people who deliberately reject God who end up in hell and not just those whom God has rejected indiscriminately.

Second Peter 3:9 NKJV states, "The Lord is not slack concerning His promise, as some count slackness, but is long-suffering toward us, not willing that any should perish but that all should come to repentance."

This verse makes a clear statement about who the Lord wants to be saved. The Lord delays His second coming to give mankind more opportunity to repent. He wants everyone saved. He doesn't wish any to perish. The Lord is full of mercy and grace, slow to anger, and full of compassion. However, we must remember that He is also a God of vengeance and wrath toward the sinner (see Psalm 5:4–5).

As it was

History will show that when any culture begins to operate without God, it travels down the road of lawlessness. It will be a slow digression and will hardly be noticed. There lies the danger. No one notices that downward slide of morality until it is too late. Whenever humanity is allowed to decide what is right or wrong for itself, it will most often decide based on whatever the newest trend in morality happens to be. Sometimes a person's view of morality is founded on what is acceptable in the society they live in rather than through the lens of Scripture. Whenever a culture holds to a wrong view of God, then lawlessness is not far behind.

> And as it was in the days of Noah, so it will also be in the days of the Son of Man: They ate, they drank, they married wives, they were given in marriage, until the day that Noah entered the ark, and the flood came and destroyed them all. Likewise, as it was also in the days of Lot: They ate, they drank, they bought, they sold, they planted, they built; but on the day that Lot went out of Sodom it rained fire and brimstone from

heaven and destroyed them all. Even so, will it
be in the day when the Son of Man is revealed.
(Luke 17:26–30 NKJV)

In Noah's day, the human race had deteriorated to the point
that everything in their imagination was evil and incessantly practiced. The thoughts of their hearts were constantly evil, even as it is in
some today. According to the words of Jesus, this present world will
continue just as it did in Noah's days because man's heart shows no
definite change for the better. Those who believe that man is good at
their core are at odds with what God's Word is teaching (see Jeremiah
17:9).

Genesis 6:5 NKJV states, "Then the LORD saw that the wickedness of man was great in the earth and that every intent of the
thoughts of his heart was only evil continually."

As in Noah's day, God's enemies are so caught up in their wicked
imaginations that they don't see their impending judgment on the
horizon. Their hearts have become hardened to the point that they
no longer see or feel the sting of sin. They accept their lifestyle as
being one of normality. This spiritual condition most often is self-in-
duced, and the desires of the flesh only strengthen it. Like those of
Noah's day, many have become drunk on their success and pleasures
to the point that they cannot receive the truth. Spiritual numbness
has set in. They see no need to change their lives; they like it just the
way it is. They are depending on the hyper-grace of religion to save
them. The opioid of the church is that a different form of grace is
being taught. True grace allows us to live free from the condemnation
of sin. False grace teaches that one can live without the fear of having to answer for a sinful lifestyle. It is a lack of reverential fear that
causes one to become an enemy.

Regrettably, the enemy of God will not pay attention to the
signs of His coming just as they ignored those in Noah's day. They
are too occupied with the affairs of life to heed the warnings. There
are plenty of signs to show before the Lord's second return, but few
people heed them. Preoccupation with the carnal realm will blind the
enemy to the realities of the spiritual realm (see Mark 4:19, 8:17).

Spiritual pride can also blind a person so that they believe that they live according to the Word of God when they live according to their flesh.

It's not what we, as sinful creatures, consider acceptable behavior that holds any bearing or weight with God. He has never asked for our opinion, nor does He need our counsel; it will be what God thinks is right or wrong. It will be the standard of God's holiness that will call every man into account for his actions. The enemy of God will forever be lost, with no opportunity to repent, if they wait till the last day. God has given every person a revelation of His holiness, so there will be no excuse to offer. One day, every unbeliever will have to stand before God and answer for the things they knew were wrong in their heart. In their hearts, they know better. In Romans 1:20, Paul said this inner witness of God causes the individual to clearly see the invisible things of God and even understand the Godhead. There can be no doubt that every person who has ever walked the earth has had a clear revelation of God. The use of the word *understood* firmly states that God gave man the understanding to use that knowledge. Man will stand before the Creator, where there will be no hiding or excuses made of his life.

> For the wrath of God is revealed from heaven against all ungodliness and unrighteousness of men, who suppress the truth in unrighteousness, because what may be known of God is manifest in them, for God has shown it to them. For since the creation of the world His invisible attributes are clearly seen, being understood by the things that are made, even His eternal power and Godhead, so that they are without excuse. (Romans 1:18–20 NKJV)

Tragically, the enemy of God sees little reason for alarm and fails to appreciate his need for accepting Christ as his Savior. In his arrogance, he judges himself against others and declares that he is doing quite well in comparison. They are cheerfully replacing God with the idol of self. This should be considered a personal attack against the Lord's authority. Religious pride often lifts one above and against God, trying to dethrone Him by exalting self. This is called idolatry. There are two ways to commit idolatry: You can worship something other than God. Or you can worship God contrary to how He has commanded us.

Thus, the enemy of God imagines himself secure and continues headlong without any thought regarding eternity. The lack of immediate judgment and God's persistent silence only increase his boldness against God. They mistakenly assume that because there are no immediate consequences for their actions, there will be no judgment when, in fact, it shows that God is planning holy retribution. God is not required to be in a hurry because He knows the sinner cannot escape Him. There is no place for the enemy of God to hide. It is only a matter of time that every man will reap what he has sown. In due time, every transgression and disobedience shall receive what is due them with the major indictment being the rejection of Jesus.

Psalm 139:7–8 NKJV states, "Where can I go from Your Spirit? Or where can I flee from Your presence? If I ascend into heaven, You are there; If I make my bed in hell, behold, You are there."

PART 2
The Wrath of God

There can be little doubt that the wrath of God shall be delivered. Paul labored to show this truth in the first part of this letter to the Romans. Paul has shown us that "the wrath of God is revealed from heaven against all ungodliness and unrighteousness of men, who by their unrighteousness suppress the truth" (Romans 1:18). The truth of God's wrath is known by all men, but not all men adhere to that truth. In Romans 1:20, Paul said this inner witness of God causes the individual to clearly understand God's wrath concerning men standing against Him. Therefore, no one will be able to stand before God on the day of judgment and say, "I didn't know." He has given all people who have ever lived, regardless of how remote or isolated they may have been, the opportunity to know His wrath. They are without excuse.

There are some points of interest that the enemy of God should consider. If God's love is pure and without restraint, then His wrath will be just as pure and unrestrained. Sin always brings justice, and the righteousness of God's judgment upon sin will be precise and exact. God's anger is not a product of emotion such as found in humanity, but one can be sure that there will be such an intensity that words cannot accurately describe.

A future time is coming when God will pour out His wrath on all the earth (see Revelation 6:17, 11:18, 14:19, 15:1, 7, 16:1, 19, 19:15). Unbelievers are presently under the wrath of the Old Testament law (see John 5:45; Romans 4:15; Galatians 3:10; John 3:18) and, unless they repent, will suffer eternally (see Romans

2:6–9; Revelation 20:13–15). Praise God that in this present age, Jesus has come not to condemn people but to bring them grace and truth (see John 1:14, 3:17). There is hope for those who will come to Christ and receive the gift of salvation. Christ came to pay our debt, not to collect it.

So the question begs, If all this is true, then why can't we observe more of this intuitive knowledge about God's wrath in the lives of those who have not heard the gospel? First, just because people claim ignorance doesn't void the fact that God has placed it there. Nobody ever told Adam that he had sinned against God, but he knew that he had. When God created the first man and first woman, He placed them in the garden of Eden, where they lived in a state of innocence, without sin. God freely gave them the fruit of every tree in the garden but one: the tree of the knowledge of good and evil. "Do not partake of that tree," God said, "for when you eat from it you will certainly die" (Genesis 2:17). Some people reason that Adam and Eve's punishment for disobedience was overly harsh because they could not have known good from evil.

But the Bible never says that Adam and Eve did not know right from wrong. In fact, Genesis 3:2–3 is clear that they did understand the difference between right and wrong. Eve knew God had instructed her and Adam not to eat the forbidden fruit (see Genesis 2:16–17). To assume that they had no knowledge of right and wrong because of "the tree of the knowledge of good and evil" (Genesis 2:9) is a total misunderstanding of the terms. In the Bible, the word *knowledge* often means "experience." Adam and Eve indeed had no experience of evil before the fall. You don't have to commit sin to understand that it is wrong. The point is that Adam and Eve had not yet sinned until they ate from the tree, and their sin was the gateway to the firsthand, experiential knowledge of the difference between good and evil.

Adam and Eve indeed, understood the difference between right and wrong, but they hadn't experienced it personally until they sinned. Their lack of experience was no excuse for their actions, nor shall it be for us. God gave a simple, straightforward instruction to

Adam and Eve. That should have been enough to follow, but they disobeyed anyway.

Yet despite all their blessings, Adam and Eve listened to the serpent, which directly contradicted what God had commanded them to do (Genesis 3:4–5). The serpent had done nothing to provide for them nor to show any love toward them. It was his only words that caused them to disobey. Satan had challenged the goodness of God they had experienced up to that point. Yet they trusted him even though it meant rejecting what they did know about God's provision and loving care. Genesis 3:5–6 demonstrates that Adam and Eve saw the fruit as an opportunity to become "like God." This idolatry continues even to this day. The enemy of God, just like Satan, desires to be the god of their own destiny.

Unfaithful

The unfaithful church member can become the enemy of God, just like the unbeliever. Both will remain as such until they repent and receive the forgiveness that the Lord has offered. Imagine the absurdity of being in opposition to the one true God, who is all-powerful and all-knowing. Only a foolish, self-deceived person would dare think that they could genuinely decide what is best for their life. An enemy's life decisions are based upon what pleases and satisfies the flesh, which is opposed to God entirely. The enemy of God thinks and conducts their lives in terms of carnality, which leads to death (Romans 8:6–8). Failure for that person is sure, and hell is guaranteed. How serious it is to know that one's eternity hangs in the balance by the decisions made here on earth. Thomas Manton spoke of man's decision-making in regards to his eternal destination by saying, [8]"A man's greatest care should be for that place where he dwelleth longest; therefore, eternity should be in his scope."

Without a doubt, it is a terrible condition for one to be an enemy to God, yet people are more afraid of repentance than they are of their sin. They become offended, even while loving believers warn them of the results of living without God's grace and forgiveness. These people will continue to live their lives as if there were no eternal consequences. When the truth is declared about what God requires, people often do not want to hear. It's because Bible truth goes against their flesh and against the grain of a culture that treats religion as an option. Though one is offended and put off by the truth, it doesn't change anything God has declared.

While the world is ever reaching and discovering new ideas and theories, the things of God seem to be growing more undefined and open-ended than ever before. Our society now is guided, not by the Word of God, but rather by the thoughts of men where nothing is right or wrong and where there is no moral compass that points to the truth. We are adrift in our own desire for freedom and are yet lost, so we begin to worship ourselves.

When any man refuses to worship God as God, he becomes shallow, deceived, and an enemy to God. He will be led by his five physical senses rather than by his spirit. And how could it be any different (see Romans 8:5)? His thoughts are not on the things of God but instead on himself. He is considered as being the "natural man," Paul mentioned in 1 Corinthians 2:14. The term *natural man* is applied to those who are not born again but can also be descriptive of unfaith people who used to follow the Lord.

Of the Spirit

The Word of God is a book written under the direction of the Holy Spirit. It is not a book written to man's intellect but to the innermost part of the man called the heart. This is why it seems so hard to understand for some. They are trying to understand spiritual matters using only their natural minds (see John 6:63). But the Word must be understood through the spirit (see 1 Corinthians 2:14). The Holy Spirit must illuminate its truths to our minds (see Proverbs 20:27). The Word is a language spoken from the heart of the Spirit to the heart of man. Therefore, it is impossible (see Ephesians 4:17) to understand spiritual concepts with only the intellect. This is why we see those who profess Christ acting as if they have never met Him.

> For those who live according to the flesh set their
> minds on the things of the flesh, but those who
> live according to the Spirit, the things of the
> Spirit. For to be carnally minded is death, but to
> be spiritually minded is life and peace. Because
> the carnal mind is enmity against God; for it is
> not subject to the law of God, nor indeed can be.
> So then, those who are in the flesh cannot please
> God. (Romans 8:5–8 NKJV)

No one excused

Regardless of all the advances in medicine, man's most significant sickness still lies within his spirit. He is destitute of any hope and lives in absolute corruption, yet he rejects the only means of life out of hand. Without Christ, there is nothing for their future but a burning punishment in hell. Regardless of social position, status, or church affiliation, no one will be excused from sin's indictment.

Ephesians 2:12 NKJV states, "That at that time you were without Christ, being aliens from the commonwealth of Israel and strangers from the covenants of promise, having no hope and without God in the world."

Humanity stands destitute before the living God and is in such a deprived condition that they cannot save themselves; they desperately need a savior because of their helplessness. No other religion can offer what is truly needed, and that being the Savior. Other religions teach that the burden of salvation is placed upon people's shoulders and measured by their good works. Since people could never redeem themselves, God paid the price Himself. No other method is acceptable to God other than faith in the Lord Jesus.

> For since the creation of the world His invisible
> attributes are clearly seen, being understood by
> the things that are made, even His eternal power
> and Godhead, so that they are without excuse,
> because, although they knew God, they did

not glorify Him as God, nor were thankful, but became futile in their thoughts, and their foolish hearts were darkened. Professing to be wise, they became fools. (Romans 1:20–22 NKJV)

The words of Jesus reveal that there would be a time when the hearts of men would grow cold and unbelieving (Matthew 24:12). Christ said that there would be a "great falling away" from true biblical faith among the people of God. After comparing scripture to what we are witnessing in society today, one can be confident that we live in the dreadful day He described. Those whose hearts are cold, stubborn, and unyielding define the unbeliever wholly. At the same time, the great falling away unquestionably denotes the church falling away from the faith. God requires both parties to repent and acknowledge their dependence on Him. Repentance occurs when the heart fills with sorrow because of the things that break God's heart. And repentance is the one thing the enemy of God refuses to do.

Hatred for God

Another characteristic of an enemy of God is that they will have an extreme hatred for God and His Word. This hatred for God will be the fuel that drives the heart. They may not exhibit their disgust in such a manner as to be noticed, but it thrives in their heart no less. Additionally, they no longer love the truth. They have no desire to live by the Bible or any truth that God is trying to impart to them. They believe that a newer, more enlightened society or a bigger government can replace God in our lives. Because of their hatred, they foolishly reject any attempt the Lord makes to rescue them. If people persist in their rebellion against this conviction of God, He will give those people up to their own hearts' lust.

When people persistently ignore the knowledge of God's wrath, He will leave them alone to live as they please without any sense of guilt. To the enemy of God, sin becomes routine and assumed as normal behavior. One of the most critical issues for those who practice such a lifestyle is that they want to regain their self-esteem lost due to sin. They desire to be thought of as ordinary and reasonable people. They genuinely believe that the way they live is acceptable when it is not according to God's Word, and they hate the fact that the truth is staring them in the face. No matter how much society approves of sin, it will never be accepted in the eyes of God.

For the enemy of God, their carnal desires are their god; meaning, they are led by their fleshly desires and appetites. They worship a god made in their own image. Excess and gain drive their life. They celebrate the things that should cause them shame, and their hearts always desire the things of this world rather than God's. Paul wept as he declared their end as destruction (see Philippians 3:18). The enemy of God becomes a person who joyfully practices wickedness. They actually *glory in their shame*. They magnify and celebrate their way of life as being normal. It is not that they have totally lost their knowledge of what is right and wrong; they simply ignore God's conviction about it. They know and understand that they practice a sinful lifestyle contrary to God's Word, but they no longer care. The sting of conviction is lost, and the conscience no longer feels the guilt. This is the strong delusion that comes upon those whose heart is set on living their life in the way they desire.

> The coming of the lawless one is according to the working of Satan, with all power, signs, and lying wonders, and with all unrighteous deception among those who perish, because they did not receive the love of the truth, that they might be saved. And for this reason God will send them strong delusion, that they should believe the lie. (2 Thessalonians 2:9–11 NKJV)

This delusion happens to those who do not love the truth. Thankfully, people who still desire to be in the right relationship with God show that Holy Spirit is still dealing with them, and hope remains alive. Andrew Wommack explains the delusion by saying, [9]"The Lord would never give people a strong delusion that would keep them from receiving salvation. The Lord is 'not willing that any perish, but that all should come to repentance' (2 Peter 3:9). When people reject the truth, He has shown them they are, in a sense, choosing deception by their own free will; He is just enforcing their own decisions. This only happens to those who don't love the truth."

While sin may give pleasure for a season, we must understand that there will be a day of reckoning before God. On that day, when all lives will be held accountable, man will be without excuse. An eternity in hell awaits those who refuse to repent of their sinful lifestyle and come to Jesus. The righteous Judge will render the verdict, and it will be exact and everlasting. There will be no acquittal or second chance. No prayers offered up will have any effect after death for the one who is found guilty. Those who reject Jesus as Savior are abandoning the only hope given for salvation forever. God's enemy's mindset is that they will "work something out" in the end, but they fail to realize that it will be too late by then. God's holy justice will be at work with the punishment of the wicked.

It is essential to know that God is not sending a person to hell for their sin alone but for not accepting Christ as Lord and Savior. God is long-suffering, but He is not forever suffering. And He will eventually allow one to live as they see fit. No one can know when that time will come except the Lord. The decisions made on the earth will determine one's eternal destination. Those who say, "Thy will be done," will receive the reward of a glorious life in heaven. Those who say, "My will be done" will spend eternity in hell. A. W. Pink, again, offered this thought on the wrath of God: [10]"Indifference to sin is a moral blemish, and he who hates it not is a moral leper. How could He who is the Sum of all excellency look with equal satisfaction upon virtue and vice, wisdom and folly? How could He who is infinitely holy disregard sin and refuse to manifest His 'severity' [see Romans 9:12] toward it?"

Again, we read as follows:

> And even as they did not like to retain God in their knowledge, God gave them over to a debased mind, to do those things which are not fitting; being filled with all unrighteousness, sex-

ual immorality, wickedness, covetousness, maliciousness; full of envy, murder, strife, deceit, evil-mindedness; they are whisperers, backbiters, haters of God, violent, proud, boasters, inventors of evil things, disobedient to parents, undiscerning, untrustworthy, unloving, unforgiving, unmerciful; who, knowing the righteous judgment of God, that those who practice such things are deserving of death, not only do the same but also approve of those who practice them. (Romans 1:28–32 NKJV)

God has made provision for man to know the difference between right and wrong through the conscience's work. The word *reveal*, as found in Romans 1:18, is defined as [11]"to make known through divine inspiration. To make [something secret or hidden] publicly or generally known means it is apparent to everyone." The heart can reject this knowledge and can become calloused to the truth of the scripture. Every person who has ever lived has the awareness placed within their heart concerning the wrath of God against unrighteousness. While the sinner is an enemy toward God, God is the enemy to sin. He is determined to punish sin, and because all men are sinners, all men are exposed to His punishment.

> [12]We will give an account one day because we are accountable, and there is a standard. God is the One before whom we are accountable, and our lives will be compared against His perfect character. This is why we feel guilty, because deep down, we know we are guilty. Our guilty feelings and sense of shame come because we have violated God's good and wise commandments. (Timothy Lane)

God intended for man's conscience to be his instrument of discernment. Adam was very aware of what pleased God and was very much aware of what God had spoken to him. Adam's conscience was working correctly because up until the fall, there was no contamination of sin. However, the nature of Adam's conscience changed when he decided to disobey the Word of God and choose his own way. The human heart, now guided by a malformed conscience, is deceitful in all its activities. We can no longer trust our sin-driven hearts because of the actions Adam took in the garden. For a man's heart to begin to function correctly, there must be a creative miracle within his spirit. He has to be born again by the work of the cross to reestablish the connection to the Father. When we are saved, the Holy Spirit comes to live within our spirit and will teach the heart of man how to live a godly life. God also requires repentance, which means that there has to be a change in lifestyle. For some, to change would require the admission of fault, and typically pride will not allow that. To justify sin, an enemy of God uses devilish, flesh-driven reasoning rather than the wisdom that comes from the Word of God.

Seared conscience

The enemy of God no longer feels any conviction about sin. They have been "desensitized" when it comes to guilt. Sin no longer gives them pause; they no longer sense the disapproval of their own conscience. The reprobate mind may even try to replace the feelings of guilt by normalizing their sin. In so doing, they could remove the sense of responsibility for their actions. However, despite their best efforts, no one will be able to say that they were not aware of God's wrath and judgment.

If one can remove the sting of guilt, then we feel that maybe we can reclaim a sense of self-respect and dignity. When this removal does not occur, then the enemy of God considers anyone who disagrees with them as backward and dogmatic. So with determination and steady resolve, the reprobate mind drives straight into the gates of damnation without any thought of payment or judgment.

First Timothy 4:1–2 KJV states, "Now the Spirit speaketh expressly, that in the latter times some shall depart from the faith, giving heed to seducing spirits, and doctrines of devils; Speaking lies in hypocrisy; having their conscience seared with a hot iron."

It troubles some people to think that God would allow one to live as they choose while knowing that their end will be destruction. Where is the mercy of God? Would a loving God send someone to their eternal destruction? Hardly so. The saving grace of Jesus clearly demonstrates God's mercies and love to us. His greatest desire is that all men would come to repentance, but He will not force anyone to accept the work of the cross. When people reject Jesus, they deny their only hope. A. W. Pink, again, has clearly defined our answer: [13]"How dreadful would it be if the present order of things, when the children of God are obliged to live in the midst of the children of the Devil, should continue forever!"

The enemy of God will refuse to submit to his Creator. He is, for all practical purposes, acting like his father, the devil. Satan is the author of rebellion. Therefore, when they against God, they are only acting out what is natural. When individuals rebel against God, they are prideful, just like Satan desired to be like God. They want to be the lord over their own life just as Satan did. When one rebels against God, they are actually trying to replace Him with their own image. This is called idolatry. By doing so, they are forsaking their freedom rather than gaining it because Satan is a heavy taskmaster.

On the other hand, when men and women submit to God, they become truly free. They receive the ability to become the remarkable, unique beings that God created them to be. Once a person comes by faith to Jesus, the power of sin has no claim on that person. Not only is the guilt removed but so is the curse of sin which is death.

Jeremiah 29:11 NKJV states, "For I know the thoughts that I think toward you, says the LORD, thoughts of peace and not of evil, to give you a future and a hope."

The Lord has a plan for each of our lives, and it contains nothing but good. Those who seek God with all their hearts will undoubtedly face problems in this world. But they are promised victory and an expected end. Many of the issues we face come because we aren't following God's plans. It's when we rebel and try to overcome by our own strength that most of us encounter trouble. As we follow God's plans for our lives, we can be assured of the outcome. There will be an expected future.

"Then you will call upon Me and go and pray to Me, and I will listen to you" (Jeremiah 29:12 NKJV). Only a rebel would consider living a life of disobedience against God. This truth also applies to the believer who has strayed away from God. Jesus has never forced anyone to get saved, nor shall He force anyone to continue.

In due time, God will deal with all those who reject Christ as an adversary. They have rejected the only one who loves them enough to die for them. The Lord views friendship with the world in the harshest of terms. In regards to the believer, it is consorting with the enemy and, therefore, treasonous. Those who desert the army of God to have fellowship with God's enemy will undoubtedly find themselves at odds with God. Living in deliberate sin is the highest crime against the greatest Being!

God's enemy lives as if the Almighty does not exist or is disinterested or, worse, as if He winks at sin because of His great love for humanity. Without question, our Father has consistently demonstrated great compassion for His creation and will continue to do so. His love and mercies have no limits and are new every day. However, it would be wise on our part to remember that while His love is pure, His wrath is just as genuine.

Most unbelievers would not think of themselves as being an enemy to God. They have created a god of their liking to soothe their conscience and justify their sin. Their god would never be displeased or angry. He would always be in a good mood and be ever approving of their actions. They would never invent a god who would judge harshly and bring punishment to the ones He loves. Neither would He allow someone to enter into hell for all eternity for "a few small indiscretions." To think this way is the height of selfishness. The very nature of self-righteousness is the worst of sins because it is rooted and grounded in unbelief and pride. The enemies of God are always self-righteous and see themselves as being good enough to judge what is to be fair and just. They depend on and trust in their works rather than what God has declared about us. According to their own standards, the enemies of God are the self-appointed judges that determine what is right and wrong.

[14]"God is indeed on a throne of grace, but that is no less glorious and suited to inspire reverence than a throne of judgment" (William Plumer, 1776).

The rebellious man will have no excuse or hope before the Judge of the Universe. On the day of reckoning, all outstanding debts shall be payable. While the judgment of God appears to be delayed, it will not be denied. His decision to punish will not be a sudden flash of anger but rather a deliberate, calculated act of righteousness. It will be so precise and articulated that it will appear that He is no longer a god of mercy.

What does the enemy look like? How can one know? Simply put, the enemy of God could be a family member or a friendly neighbor living across the street. At face value, they pose no threat to society. They can be moral and upright and so ethically sound that they do not sense the need for Jesus. They may even be a member of a local church. Nonetheless, what is going to count on judgment day is their relationship with Jesus. If they are not members of the family of God through the sacrifice of Jesus, they are now and will remain the enemy of God until they repent.

> [15]You call Me master, and obey Me not; You call Me light, and see Me not; You call Me the way, and walk Me not; You call Me life, and live Me not; You call Me wise, and follow Me not; You call Me fair, and love Me not; You call Me rich, and ask Me not; You call Me eternal, and seek Me not. If I condemn thee, blame Me not. (Author unknown)

Understanding holiness

We need not look too far to see with certainty that the definition of holiness and righteousness has changed with modern times and with the tides of an ever-shifting culture. Every day that passes brings a lower level of immorality, moving ever deeper into spiritual darkness and further from the standards of holiness that God set. The world and the church, in some instances, act as if the Lord has somehow modified His definition of holiness or lessened His requirements to accommodate man's bent heart.

God's standard of holiness will stand for the ages because the Eternal One spoke it out of the spirit realm. The philosophy and viewpoint of man can never alter the meaning of holiness. Neither the opinions of the intellectual nor the progressive liberal teachings in the higher educational institutions of the land can interpret God's intent on the subject of holiness. Who is man to think that he can modify what God has decreed? To oppose the Word of God is to resist God Himself, and this qualifies one to be an enemy of God.

Sadder still is the fact that not only is the unbeliever at odds with the Almighty but also are those who, at one time, called themselves Christian. They may go through the motions of religion, but they have no life evidence of ever coming to terms with Jesus. The church member can live as they see fit just as much as the nonbeliever and should expect the same rewards. Having one's name on the church roll does not give an exemption to God's standards. As stated before, He will not excuse anyone from this indictment regardless of their social position, status, or ministry affiliation. It could be the rich man who wants nothing or the pauper who struggles daily for every necessity or the academic scholar with degrees in philosophy or the uneducated laborer. No one receives immunity.

Galatians 6:7–8 NKJV states, "Do not be deceived, God is not mocked; for whatever a man sows, that he will also reap. For he who sows to his flesh will of the flesh reap corruption, but he who sows to the Spirit will of the Spirit reap everlasting life."

The believer's responsibility is to renew his mind to "observe to do all that is written therein" (see Joshua 1:8 NKJV). It's important to learn to renew our minds so that we can live a holy life acceptable to the Almighty. Whenever we fail in our responsibility to renew the mind toward God, we run the risk of becoming the enemy of God. The belief of "Once saved, always saved" has no scriptural basis. Living for God is a daily decision that falls squarely on the shoulders of every believer. God will not perform what He has commanded a man to do, nor shall He allow man to accomplish what He holds for Himself. The eternal end of a person who once received salvation but now has rejected Christ is infinitely worse than before they got saved (see Hebrews 6:4–6).

Romans 12:1–2 NKJV states, "I beseech you therefore, brethren, by the mercies of God, that you present your bodies a living sacrifice, holy, acceptable to God, which is your reasonable service. And do not be conformed to this world, but be transformed by the renewing of your mind, that you may prove what is that good and acceptable and perfect will of God."

No difference

God will not judge the unfaithful church member in a different the unbeliever regarding being continue in a sinful lifestyle. If that person lives as though they have never met Jesus, they are in the same predicament as the unbeliever. Jesus addressed those who claimed to be His disciples by saying that He never knew them.

Matthew 7:23 KJV states, "And then will I profess unto them, I never knew you: depart from me, ye that work iniquity."

What an indictment against the one who trusts he is safe but reality has no right standing with God. Think about the term "I *never* knew you." To understand what Jesus was saying here, we must realize the omniscience of Christ. That is to say "all-knowing." He is God, and, therefore, nothing is unknown to Him. Christ knew they existed, and He knew their character and their works. But despite all their efforts, the Lord called them *workers of iniquity*. They had been doing the ministry's work all under the appearance of religion and all for nothing. However, God considers the motive and intent of the heart. He knew the reason for all their actions, and nothing is hidden from Him. Christ said, "I never made any account of you as a disciple of mine, as belonging to me; I never approved of you nor your conduct. I have never known you through My Father's covenant of grace. You never believed in me, loved me, or obeyed My word. Therefore, I will have nothing to do with you."

We must remember that James addressed the church concerning being an enemy to God and not those living outside of the church. Being faithful and loyal to the King is a requirement for entering the kingdom of God. When a person's loyalty turns toward the world and not toward God, they become an enemy. As life centers around themselves, they become traitors to the King and not fit for the kingdom. To this kind, God is no more than a jack-in-the-box helper that they can easily access in times of trouble. To drive home the point, James used the terms *adulteress* and *adulterers*. James shows us that one can become unfaithful to God and break the covenant by referring to marital unfaithfulness. God is not the one who breaks the bonds of covenant. He will never leave or abandon us, but that is not the same as a man abandoning God. No sin, other than blaspheming the Holy Ghost, is unforgivable. All sin is terrible and carries a penalty in itself, but the greatest is the rejection of Christ. Still, God forbid that there should be anyone who feels that they have sinned past the forgiveness and mercy of God. His mercies are new every day, and there is no limit to His grace. No, if you genuinely repent and realize the error of your sin and call upon the boundless love, mercy, and grace of God, you can be forgiven, and then you should "go and sin no more."

How can it be that holiness standards are left up to the fickle impulses of an ever-changing society? Do we allow those who have the most influence over our nation to determine what righteous living standards should be? By doing so, we are allowing a blind man to lead someone with eyesight across the road. The worldly man has no authority to tell the child of God how to live, and the child of God has no business holding to the principles of the world. We are to be different. We are not to be as those in the world.

Horizontal thinking people are afraid of not being accepted while here on earth. They are continually striving for what the world has to offer but seldom reaching the goal. The driving force behind a sinful life is selfishness. Idolatry is the end result of this kind of life where we become what we think God should be like. God didn't create us to be rejected but to be accepted, and that's the reason we have an inborn desire to fit in. Peer pressure and the fear of being rejected will cause you to conform to the world. But Christ not only saved you from the guilt of your sin but also from the power of sin over your life. If you live a life separate from that of the world, then God will accept you.

Second Corinthians 6:17 NKJV states, "Therefore, 'Come out from among them And be separate, says the Lord. Do not touch what is unclean, And I will receive you.'"

The body of Christ needs to recognize that the unregenerate man has always loved the darkness and has consistently shunned the light of truth. It is in his nature to act in such a way. He prizes the dark and considers it his home, so when the light of truth is shown, they become uncomfortable and offended. The Word of God tells us that light and darkness can have no fellowship. There can be no gray areas in one's life. Man can conceal his heart for a time, but once exposed to the light, he must decide whether to continue in the ways of the world or choose the Word of God.

John 3:19–21 NKJV states, "And this is the condemnation, that the light has come into the world, and men loved darkness rather than light because their deeds were evil. For everyone practicing evil hates the light and does not come to the light, lest his deeds should be exposed."

In our nation today, we can see those who have the most influence are now setting the standards of righteous living based on today's latest social trends. Our highest courts attempt to legislate morality from the bench. Meanwhile, the progressives have declared that the Bible is old-fashioned and dated; they have declared the Bible irrelevant to the times.

In some cases, liberal and open-minded messages are being taught in some so-called Christian universities. Students are being shown more than simple tolerance towards a different culture but unconditional acceptance of sin. The world has changed the definition of tolerance from respect and forbearance to mean, unqualified approval and endorsement of others' beliefs as the truth. This belief is the beginning of pluralism, which teaches that we must embrace our differences, regardless of any immorality to make ourselves stronger. Jesus warned us of the leaven of the Pharisees.

Matthew 16:6 NKJV states, "Then Jesus said to them, 'Take heed and beware of the leaven of the Pharisees and the Sadducees.'"

Carnal-minded

How often do we miss the point because we are so carnally minded (see Romans 8:6–7; 1 Corinthians 2:14)? This scripture gives a stern warning to those who think others' opinions and doctrines cannot harm them. As Paul said in 1 Corinthians 15:33, we are deceived if we believe others' communication cannot affect us. The evil doctrine of pluralism will almost always be hidden by the religious thoughts of men. Some would argue that good always overcomes evil, but that is simply not the case. We are not to live a reclusive lifestyle; however, we cannot associate wholly with the world. Jesus was a friend to the sinner, but He never took part in their sin. We would do well to follow His example.

Carnal-mindedness does not just have a tendency to lead toward death, but it also equals death. Death in the scripture is much more than the physical end of life. Death is being disconnected from God. It also includes sickness, depression, anger, poverty, and anything else resulting from sin. To be spiritually minded is life and peace. Carnal people think and act carnally because they think only in terms of self. They have separated themselves from the only hope that is available by their rejection of Jesus. Accordingly, the results of being an enemy of God will cost them in the end.

> For to be carnally minded is death, but to be spiritually minded is life and peace. Because the carnal mind is enmity against God; for it is not subject to the law of God, nor indeed can be. So then, those who are in the flesh cannot please God. (Romans 8:6–8 NKJV)

Pluralism

It seems that the prevailing winds of change are blowing traditional bible doctrine into the areas of pluralism. Pluralism is defined as "not one word of sound moral doctrine measured only by the Word of God." The only thing that pluralism rejects is rejection itself. This philosophy declares that there are many ways to God. There is no one absolute truth, and any truth accepted depends on the individual. Having a pluralistic mindset leads one to believe that guilt is a personal choice rather than necessary accountability. The Apostle Paul warned us of the day in which we live by emphasizing the warning with "But know this."

> But know this, that in the last days perilous times will come: For men will be lovers of themselves, lovers of money, boasters, proud, blasphemers, disobedient to parents, unthankful, unholy, unloving, unforgiving, slanderers, without self-control, brutal, despisers of good, traitors, headstrong, haughty, lovers of pleasure rather than lovers of God, having a form of godliness but denying its power. And from such people turn away! (2 Timothy 3:1–5 NKJV)

The Word of God consistently commands the believer not to live like the world. Jesus saved us not only from our sin but also from the course of the world. God's insistence that we live differently from the world poses the question, What exactly is the world? In general, the term *world* can refer to planet earth. However, the Bible refers to *the world* as the corrupt moral system controlled by Satan that leads us away from the worship of God (see 2 Corinthians 4:4). It also relates to the humanistic method of religion that is in opposition to the standards of God. When the Bible says, "For God loved the world," it refers to the human beings who live here. Jesus did not die for the physical planet but for those who are created in His image. While academics may disagree on the meaning of the word *world*, it stands clear in the scripture that anything that opposes the Word of God is not of God and therefore is of the world.

[16]"Worldliness is what any particular culture does to make sin look normal, and righteousness looks strange" (David Wells).

Those who demonstrate affections for the offerings of the world are not the friends of God. It is not the believer who falls into sin occasionally who becomes God's enemy. Instead, the enemies of God are those who call themselves Christian yet have deep affection and desire for the world's things. Without repentance, grace has no place to work. God never intended for anyone to accept the gift of salvation through the work of Jesus only to continue to live like the world. The Father's desire was for man to act as His ambassador on the earth. Instead, we have become the ambassador of the devil.

[17]"Every man, by his own natural will, hates God; but when he is turned to the Lord, by evangelical repentance, then his will is changed" (George Whitfield).

Where does the western church stand in all this today? It seems that some have assumed the responsibility of setting the standards of how to live a Christian life. We alter things, such as worship, without consulting Christ, who has been given all supremacy over everything. Is it true that we have a form of godliness but no power? Are we now weak and frail and helpless to defend our beliefs? Do we allow the spirit of rebellion to live among us as comfortably as it does with the unbeliever? Maybe the ministers that preach need to examine their heart before any change can be expected.

The message of the postmodern church no longer deals with sin or repentance as it once did. Biblical church discipline, according to scripture, is no longer practiced. Regarding the latter, we should not conduct witch hunts in order to cleanse the church of sinners. But we should not be afraid to deal with it biblically when it presents itself. Many have attempted to maintain a social balance when dealing with sin issues within the body of Christ, but this is contrary to scripture (see John 13:34–35; 1 Corinthians 5:11). I believe issues concerning sin are often overlooked or ignored out of convenience, fear, and accommodation. We are to love the fellowship enough to help them recover themselves. If they refuse to repent, then there is no other alternative than to remove that person from the fellowship of the church.

In our day, so many ministers are teaching half-truths as being the whole. When half of the message of Christ is preached, then all the listeners are in danger. The misunderstanding or abuse of God's grace has led many to accept tolerance to sin. The new message offers salvation to everyone without ever mentioning dying to self or taking up the cross of Jesus. Discipleship often is seen as an *option* rather than a mandate. Actions and speech once viewed as vulgar and indecent are now standard behavior and acceptable in the body of Christ. Sacred doctrine is no longer profitable; therefore, it is not preached as a way of life but rather as a range of options.

Isaiah 5:20–21 NKJV states, "Woe to those who call evil good, and good evil; Who put darkness for light, and light for darkness; Who put bitter for sweet, and sweet for bitter! Woe to those who are wise in their own eyes, And prudent in their own sight!"

Some have accepted the false notion that God loves us and receives us just as we are so long as we regularly attend services. Over time and for the sake of convenience, we permit false doctrine to creep into our teachings without any criticism. Many will perish because no one speaks up, including those responsible for watching (see Ezekiel 33:1–6). Ministers are the spiritual watchmen for the people of God. We are called and equipped to alert the people of an invading army; it is our responsibility to counsel people about the dangers of neglecting God's Word. As ministers of the gospel, we must understand that our appointment as watchmen comes from God and not from a man. It is not our obligation to make anyone respond, but they can't return to God if they are not warned.

One Master

Jesus tells us—the believer—that we cannot serve two masters (see Matthew 6:24). We will love the one and hate the other, but we cannot be servants to both. God requires us to choose Him or the world. To stay in a neutral position is to be lukewarm in the eyes of Jesus. A person in an uncommitted condition is no better than a person who has never accepted Christ. This approach to Christianity is in direct violation of what Paul commanded in his letter to Corinth's church.

Second Corinthians 6:14 NKJV states, "Do not be unequally yoked together with unbelievers. For what fellowship has righteousness with lawlessness? And what communion has light with darkness?"

To enter into the kingdom of God, one must move past being simply intellectually connected to Christ. It will not be the one who simply believes in God who will go to heaven. Only the true disciple will enter into the kingdom. The devil believes in God, so just having a required belief in God falls short of God's requirements. Every soul who has died without Christ now believes in God but has no hope of receiving Him because of their prior decision to reject Him. The church of modern times has somehow separated the word *punishment* from eternity, giving a false sense of reality. The most prevailing thought any human should have should be about where they will spend eternity. The images of hell found in the Bible are terrible, and I am confident that whatever we read will pale in comparison to reality. One characteristic is the separation from God. While it is true that a person will face being separated from God, but that does not mean that his dealing with God is finally over. That person will remain guilty before a holy God and suffer His holy wrath with no end. Thus, the person who is consigned to hell will live with their conscience, knowing that they didn't have to come to this place. Their sentence will continue forever and ever, with no end in sight.

Moreover, it is essential for the believer to become a disciple. Jesus said that we are to teach others to observe all things, which is the same as discipleship. If the believer confesses Christ but fails to renew their mind and heart, they are more likely to go back to the things of the world. Salvation is more than just saying that Jesus is the Christ; there must be corresponding actions to one's faith in Christ.

[18]"Genuine faith must go beyond the mere intellectual assent concerning biblical doctrines. People must let the implications of these doctrines radically affect their hearts so that they respond positively to God with the obedience and works of faith" (Daniel Fuller).

Discipleship

The idea of being a disciple is to be like Jesus. Christians are to live their lives in such a way that others can see Him through their daily walk. Jesus is expecting every believer to model every area of their life by His example. By accepting Christ, we are to seek Him as our Lord and not only as our Savior. Jesus is the one who tells us how to live, how to walk, and how to talk. His only requirement is that we are to be wholly committed to Him. Jesus rebuked the church at Laodicea about being half-heartedly committed to Him while leaning on their own success.

Revelation 3:15–16 NKJV states, "I know your works, that you are neither cold nor hot. I could wish you were cold or hot. So then, because you are lukewarm, and neither cold nor hot, I will vomit you out of My mouth."

The Gospel of Jesus Christ in the western world at times seems vague, lost, and at best confused. Nowadays, many of the messages are merely informative self-help talks about God, while Spirit-driven messages about repentance, obedience, and discipleship are no longer in style. The church has become more tolerant of certain sins than others because the biblical standard for living holy has not been presented strong enough to offend the listener.

Where is the fire of the Holy Spirit in the ministry today? Has the church succumbed to a watered-down version of the gospel? When people stubbornly reject God and His righteous ways, there will always be a heavy price to pay, and we are not the one who determines the price of that sin. A. W. Pink had this to say about not preaching the true gospel:

> [19]The nature of Christ's salvation is woefully misrepresented by the present-day evangelist. He announces a Savior from hell rather than a Savior from sin. And that is why so many are fatally deceived, for there are multitudes who wish to escape the Lake of Fire who have no desire to be delivered from their carnality and worldliness.

In today's carnally engineered society, holiness is a relative term. A person now has the freedom to decide for themselves what is acceptable and what is not. Holiness now lies camouflaged under the definition of Christian liberty. The simple convert can now view bearing one's cross to follow Jesus as an unnecessary challenge rather than an obligation. However, as born-again believers, we have only one choice.

First Peter 1:15–17 NKJV states, "But as He who called you is holy, you also be holy in all your conduct, because it is written, 'Be holy, for I am holy.' And if you call on the Father, who without partiality judges according to each one's work, conduct yourselves throughout the time of your stay here in fear."

The opioid crisis of the church is that many are not speaking the truth in love so as not to offend. But instead, they are preaching a diluted, socially modified version of the gospel that leaves the listener comfortable and unoffended. The results produce listeners who are not grieved at the condition of their heart because they do not think anything is wrong. Weak disciples come from diluted ministers who deliver diluted messages. Vance Havner was quoted saying, [20]"The devil will let a preacher prepare a sermon if it will keep him from preparing himself."

The Bible speaks clearly concerning the judgment of God. We can see that now is the time for judgment to begin at the house of God (see 1 Peter 4:17). This verse makes a clear difference between the opinion of believers and unbelievers. If those who have received the grace of God are judged, then how severe will God's punishment be on those who have rejected God's offer of salvation?

The definition of sin has been changed to lessen the blow of the truth. Therefore, holiness takes on a different description. Suppose preachers do not identify sin for what it is. In that case, people cannot correctly respond to their condition, if they respond at all. Moreover, ministers who fail to warn others of their spiritual health will have the blood of those people on their hands (see Ezekiel 33:6). God charges ministers with accountability for half-truth preaching much in the same way we bring accusations to a medical doctor for malpractice.

His watchmen are blind, They are all ignorant;
They are all dumb dogs, They cannot bark;

Sleeping, lying down, loving to slumber. Yes, they are greedy dogs That never have enough. And they are shepherds Who cannot understand; They all look to their own way, Every one for his own gain, From his own territory. "Come," one says, "I will bring wine, And we will fill ourselves with intoxicating drink; Tomorrow will be as today, And much more abundant." (Isaiah 56:10–12 NKJV)

Society and religion both try to lessen the sting of sin by labeling it differently than it is. The wickedness of sexual lust is now "an addiction." Instead of using the term *adultery*, we prefer the term *affair* when confronting that particular sin when, in fact, they are the same transgression.

First John 3:6 states, "No one who abides in him keeps on sinning; no one who keeps on sinning has either seen him or known him."

All Christians will fall into sin on occasion, but they cannot stay in that condition. Their hearts will suffer godly sorrow, which leads to repentance. The mercy and grace of God will then cleanse them from the stain of sin. Heartfelt repentance allows the grace of God to work. Therefore, Grace and mercy cannot work without the foundation of repentance. The disciple of Christ fights the same battles as the unbeliever. Still, the power of the Holy Spirit has given them the ability of the Holy Spirit to live a holy life pleasing to God. When the believer falls into sin, he will be grieved to the heart and quickly repent because his greatest desire is to please his heavenly Father. God then quickly forgives, and the man is restored as if the sin had never occurred.

In many cases, the average believer looks like the average nonbeliever. If there is no fruit of repentance or change in the way they live, then one can safely question the authenticity of their salvation. A person may go through the requirements of religion but still have no real heart change. Only God can indeed know a person's heart, but He did say that we could identify the tree by the fruit (see Luke 6:44 NKJV).

First Peter 4:17 NKJV states, "For the time has come for judgment to begin at the house of God; and if it begins with us first, what will be the end of those who do not obey the Gospel of God?"

We must understand that those who oppose God become the enemy of God. However, James also says the Lord gives even more grace to those who will humble themselves and return to Him. Grace does not come to those who are not willing to humble themselves. God will always seek out those of a contrite spirit and a broken heart. He is merciful to those who are empty of themselves. Our Father desires more than anything to show you mercy and extend grace toward your life.

> But He gives more grace. Therefore, He says: "God resists the proud, but gives grace to the humble." Therefore submit to God. Resist the devil, and he will flee from you. (James 4:6–7 NKJV)

The heart of the gospel is love, and we are not to totally isolate ourselves from those who do not live as we do. Christians should be friends with non-Christians, but we are not to participate in or condone their lifestyle. Christ Himself associated with sinners and saints alike, and He is our example. How can the sinner be saved if the Christian remains isolated from the very ones who need Jesus the most?

There are reasons we are told not to love the world. For one, the Word of God reveals Satan as the god of this world, who operates his perverted value system wherever he is allowed. His method will always be opposed to the standard of God (see 2 Corinthians 4:4). So if we love the world, we hate God and serve Satan. That may appear to be a strong statement for some, but it is the truth. Jesus bears witness to the fact.

Matthew 6:24 KJV states, "No man can serve two masters: for either he will hate the one, and love the other, or else he will hold to the one, and despise the other. Ye cannot serve God and mammon."

For the believer to live the life of Christ, there must be a change in our lives' very essence, not just behavior modification. If we only change our behavior, we will always go back to what is genuinely in our hearts. The abundance of the heart will always dictate how we live. Suppose we consistently and deliberately practice sin after learning the truth and coming to Christ. In that case, we act in rebellion against God, which is also the same as witchcraft (see 1 Samuel 15:23 KJV). And if this is the case then we can become the enemies of God in due time.

Disobedient living was never in the supreme plan of God. It was never His intention for man to choose between good and evil, yet He has given us the ability to choose. Having the authority to choose separates humanity from all creation, including the angels, and it comes with a weighty responsibility. The angelic beings certainly could choose, but they did not have God's permission to do so.

On the other hand, man has been given the ability and the authority to choose whether or not he would obey God or rebel against God. Adam had the choice to obey God or rebel and chose rebellion. Sadly humanity is still bent on living life in a manner that seems right to him without regard to what the scriptures say.

Being an enemy to God comes down to the principle of authority. Watchman Nee explains authority this way:

> [21]The acts of God issue from His throne and His throne is established on His Authority. All things are created through God's authority, and all physical laws of the universe are maintained by His authority. Hence the Bible expresses it as "upholding all things by His word of His power," which means upholding all things by the word of the power of His authority. For God's authority represents God Himself, whereas His power stands only for His act. Sin against power is more easily forgiven than sin against His authority. The latter is a sin against God Himself. God alone is authority in all things; all the authorities on earth are instituted by God. Authority is a tremendous thing in the universe-nothing overshadows it. It

is, therefore, imperative for us who desire to serve
God to know the authority of God.

Some believe that because of the love of God, God accepts them and their sinful lifestyle. This may be true in the sense that God will receive the sinner. But He will not receive their sin. Thank God that the Word says that "while we were yet sinners, Christ died for us" (see Romans 5:8) and His love has not changed. God has always had compassion and pity for the sinner, but He cannot tolerate sin. He is a holy God, and sin cannot come into His presence. Both sinner and saint alike will stand before the throne of God and give an account for their lives. The difference between the two goes back to the blood of Jesus. Without the cleansing power of the blood of Jesus's blood, the unrepented will be in danger of eternal damnation. Just because we see no damnation now does not mean there is none.

The Word of God details precisely what Satan's system promotes: the lust of the flesh, the lust of the eyes, and the boastful pride of life. Every sin imaginable can be summed up in those three evils. Envy, adultery, pride, dishonesty, selfishness, and more spring from those three roots.

John Calvin said, [22]"The human heart is an idol factory." Idols can be anything or anyone. In today's society, we have professional athletes, actors, and actresses who have become role models for our youth and adults alike. The unquenchable desire for more things, bigger houses, and higher self-fulfillment comes at a high price that can cost that person their eternal destination with God.

Anything or anyone who controls the heart's desire can become an idol (see 1 Corinthians 10:31). The secret, hidden sins of the heart that are most dear to the owner have already become an idol. It can be hard to abandon the heart's hidden idols because of the flesh-driven satisfaction and self-vindication they can bring. Even personal tragedies and hurts can become idols if we allow them to occupy more time and space in our hearts than God.

We can admire others' skills and talents, but there can only be room in the heart for one. Those people of celebrity status are quick to promote themselves to be more than they are. Herod was such a person. When the people began to shout, "The voice of a god and not of a man!" they were simply flattering him to win his favor by appealing to his overinflated ego. It is very doubtful that these people were so impressed with Herod's speech that they proclaimed that he was a god. Herod accepted their worship, and this brought a swift reply from God (see Acts 12:22 NKJV).

Pride feeds the ego, and thus becoming an idol which can lead others down the wrong road. Loving the world not only puts us at odds with God but also worships the ruler of this world (see 1 Corinthians 10:7, 14). So while scripture commands us to love the people of the world, we must be suspicious of desires that seem to compete with God for our highest affections. We were made to worship Him alone. Our salvation is given because God desires our worship. The Word of God describes Him as a jealous God. This Godly jealousy is a positive attribute poured out on man out of unconditional mercy, unlike the sin of jealousy, which is based on selfish motives.

Those who love the world will often applaud and even celebrate sin. Those of celebrity status and influence often encourage us to envy those who live outside of the standards of God. But suppose we reject what they believe to be acceptable and progressive. In that case, they insist that we are ill-informed, backward, and intolerant. Quite often, the lives of the rich and famous stir up a spirit of dissatisfaction with our own lives.

There is nothing wrong with enjoying life and having our needs met. But there is a danger of being too earthly minded because of wrong focus. It is essential to keep the right priorities in life to follow His will.

Romans 8:6 says, "For to be carnally minded is death, but to be spiritually minded is life and peace."

Philippians 3:18–19 (NKJV) states, "For many walk, of whom I have told you often, and now tell you even weeping, that they are the enemies of the Cross of Christ: whose end is destruction, whose God is their belly, and whose glory is in their shame—who set their mind on earthly things."

That sounds very descriptive of many so-called Christians today! Little wonder the church has difficulty with its message and its mission. Does modern Christianity look that much different from the world? Do we incorporate marketing strategies of the world to increase our membership? Are we counterculture, or do we stand by the fires of the enemy while we pretend to follow Christ?

It is foolish to think that we can use man-made methods to build a Spirit-led, God-breathed church. We are created by God to be a growing, thriving organism of people empowered by the Holy Spirit, with a passion for Christ and His kingdom. Man was not involved in the designing or the development of God's redeeming plan. Salvation is the result of God's mercy and grace coming straight out of our Father's heart. His plan needs no refinement. Mercy arises solely from God's holy nature and pleasure, and man need not think that it can be improved upon.

> For to be carnally minded is death, but to be spiritually minded is life and peace. Because the carnal mind is enmity against God; for it is not subject to the law of God, nor indeed can be. So then, those who are in the flesh cannot please God. (Romans 8:6–8 NKJV)

Our natural tendency to love things to excess has drifted over from the secular world into the religious world. Can Christ be pleased with our efforts? Are we becoming too friendly with the world? When worldly people come to church, they come looking for something that cannot be found elsewhere. They should find something different than what they can see in the world. Paul did not give the believers at Corinth what they wanted but what they needed—the crucified and resurrected Jesus (see 1 Corinthians 2:6). It is impossible to preach the Word of God and the world's methods at the same time. There has to be a difference.

When we come to Christ, we are supposed to be leaving the world's way of living and thinking. The very essence of repentance is forsaking the world's system. Ministers have done the sinner an injustice by preaching Jesus as the escape from hell when He, in fact, provides an escape from sin's bondage. There has to be a change not only in our behavior but also in our very being. Salvation is a heart event through the Holy Spirit's power, which causes us to seek out and live according to what God has given us. Jesus came to release men from the control of sin, thereby freeing us from the grip of hell.

Repentance is more than simple behavior modification; it is instead a change of one's heart. It is essential to know that God's saving grace cannot work without genuine repentance. If we do not repent of our sin, God cannot bless us in our walk with Him. It seems that there is more fear of repentance than of sin. There must be repentance, and that means turning one's back toward the world and what it has to offer.

> [23]Confession by itself is not repentance. Confession moves the lips; repentance moves the heart. Naming an act as evil before God is not the same as leaving it. Though your confession may be honest and emotional, it is not enough unless it expresses a true change of heart. (Jim Elliff)

When we accept Christ by faith, we receive the ability to escape the world's passions and lust. We become members of another family. We become "new creations." Our desires turn toward Jesus. We begin by renewing our minds to think as Christ thinks. We begin to see things from an eternal perspective, and our treasures are not stored upon this earth but rather in the infinite realm of heaven. We realize that the elements and situations of this life are only temporal, and we stop loving the things and the ways of this world. When we continue to enjoy the world as the unbelievers do, our spiritual growth renders us fruitless for God's kingdom (see Matthew 3:8; Luke 6:43–45; John 15:1–8). In the end, we can become the enemies of God as well.

In John 12:25, Jesus took this thought a step further when He said, "Anyone who loves their life will lose it, while anyone who hates their life in this world will keep it for eternal life." Not loving the world extends to our own lives as well. Jesus said that we are not worthy of Him if we love anything more than Him (see Matthew 10:37–38).

There are many reasons given in the Bible as to why we should not love the world. Here are a few:

1. To love the world is the loss of the soul.

> Then Jesus said to His disciples, "If anyone desires to come after Me, let him deny himself, and take up his Cross, and follow Me. For whoever desires to save his life will lose it, but whoever loses his life for My sake will find it. For what profit is it to a man if he gains the whole world and loses his own soul? Or what will a man give in exchange for his soul?" (Matthew 16:24–26 NKJV)

Our eternal souls are priceless, yet many people have traded their eternal destination for this life's temporal pleasures. They have forgotten that one's spirit will spend forever in eternity, either in heaven or in hell. There is nothing that this world can offer to a man that will compare to what a future in heaven will be. Once we enter into the realm of eternity, there will be no recovery if we have made a mistake in our choosing. God will make no exceptions for those who find themselves in a tormenting flame. Thomas Watson described eternity by saying, [24]"Eternity to the godly is a day that has no sunset; eternity to the wicked is a night that has no sunrise."

It is impossible to define or conceive what eternity really means. It is a place where there is no way to mark time because there is none to mark. It is the eternal state of "now" with no possibility of change. While there may be a beginning to eternity, there is no end, and to not consider this fact is to be shallow and shortsighted.

2. The world hates Christ.

> John 15:18 (NKJV) states, "If the world hates you,
> you know that it hated Me before it hated you."

This scripture reveals how the Lord views our friendship with the world. He considers it adultery and fraternizing with the enemy. Those who fellowship with God's enemy find themselves in trouble with God. We cannot serve a divided Christ. He demands that we worship Him as Lord and Savior of our lives. We cannot expect to live as the world lives and have access to God's blessings. Any unfaithful relationship will produce trouble on this earth. So it stands to reason that the God of all creation should expect the same and more.

Sinners run from the light of God today the same way that Adam ran. People fight against those who bring the true light of God because they don't want their sins exposed. This is the cause of all persecution. The enemies of God have knowledge of the light, but they refuse to walk in it. They choose to walk in the darkness so that they might do the works of darkness. They are disobedient to God's Word, refuse the mercy offered to them, and stand condemned to hell. Because of their decision to rebel against God, their damnation comes from themselves.

John 3:19–20 NKJV states, "And this is the condemnation, that the light has come into the world, and men loved darkness rather than light, because their deeds were evil. For everyone practicing evil hates the light and does not come to the light, lest his deeds should be exposed."

3. The Holy Spirit forbids us.

> Do not love the world or the things in the world.
> If anyone loves the world, the love of the Father is
> not in him. For all that is in the world—the lust
> of the flesh, the lust of the eyes, and the pride of
> life—is not of the Father but is of the world. And
> the world is passing away, and the lust of it; but

he who does the will of God abides forever. (1 John 2:15–17 NKJV)

Those who love the world do not love God; it is that simple. Yet humankind will try to twist the scripture to say something different to justify their sinful lifestyle. Likewise, those who love God do not love the world or the things the world offers because the two are incompatible. The Bible tells us that we have the privilege to choose who will be our god. This decision-making process has not changed. If we decide to serve God, He will bless and save us from the day of judgment. If we choose the world and all it offers, He will allow that, but the outcome will be vastly different.

Jesus explains quite clearly the choices that we have.

Matthew 7:13–14 NKJV states "Enter by the narrow gate; for wide is the gate and broad is the way that leads to destruction, and there are many who go in by it. Because narrow is the gate and difficult is the way which leads to life, and there are few who find it."

We are told by Jesus to enter by the narrow gate. Therefore, the criticism about Christians being "narrow-minded" is appropriate. If we enter through the narrow gate, we must be narrow-minded when it applies to living biblically. There aren't multiple ways to God; there is only one way: through faith in Jesus as our personal Savior (see John 14:6). As Jesus went on to explain in Luke 13:25, some will not genuinely seek salvation until it is too late. The religious will certainly "have a zeal of God" and will try to enter by their own righteousness. But if they have not submitted themselves unto the righteousness of God (see Romans 10:2–3), their hope is in vain. Others may have mental assent to Jesus, but if they do not believe from their hearts, then they are no better off (see Luke 6:46; Romans 10:10).

4.   Repentance is required.

The Word speaks of two kinds of sorrow: one being godly and the other one being worldly. Godly sorrow will lead to life, while the latter leads to death, as it never grieves from the heart. The unrepentant only mourns for the loss of sin's pleasure instead of being broken because of sin. Godly sorrow, however, comes because the heart realizes that God, and God alone, is grieved because of sin (see Psalm 51:4 NKJV). By admitting the guilt of sin and repenting, God will forgive and restore the individual back into fellowship with Him.

Today's society has been taught to reject all "negative" emotions and develop only a positive attitude in order to overcome inevitable failures in our life. However, God gave us sorrow for our own good, and it is profitable to feel sadness at our failures if we apply the lessons learned from the sin properly. He wants us to truly repent of our actions and learn so that fellowship can be restored. Genuine repentance will cause you to hate the offense with all your heart just as He does. We should allow this sorrowfulness to draw us back to God to receive forgiveness and the cleansing of our sin. True repentance will always take you to a deeper level of fellowship with God and not just a return to normal.

Second Corinthians 7:10 NKJV states, "For godly sorrow produces repentance leading to salvation, not to be regretted. Still, the sorrow of the world produces death."

There is a danger in not repenting and accepting the work of Jesus because God will not always strive with man. He will ultimately give people over to their own destruction through their own debased and immoral thinking. When this takes place, there is no hope of salvation. The words of our Lord show us that "no man can come to me [Christ], except the Father that sent me draw him" (see John 6:44). His words are explicit and leave no room for misinterpretation or misunderstanding. Without the drawing, convicting power of the Holy Spirit, no one would ever have any desire for God.

When the Holy Spirit stops persuading a person to come to the Father, the Lord has given them over to a reprobate mind. At which time, they cannot ever be saved (see Romans 1:28). The definition of a reprobate mind draws a mental picture of the enemy of God. Consider the following description: "A morally corrupt person, one who is predestined to damnation, morally unprincipled; shameless— rejected by God and without hope of salvation, to abandon to eternal damnation."

When men and women reject the truth, they are accepting deception by default. But no matter how we try, God cannot be deceived by our hearts. He is the all-knowing God that sees directly into our motives, our intentions, and our plans. The Holy Spirit can discern the motive of our hearts even if we close our spiritual eyes to the truth. One issue the enemy of God has is that the enemy doesn't want to see the sin in his life. He chooses to enjoy sin for a season rather than repentance. Sin will bring pleasure to our senses and to our flesh, but at best, it will be short-lived. By rejecting the truth, the enemy of God will suffer for their sin for all eternity unless they come to Jesus in repentance and receive Him as Lord and Savior. It is a rebellious spirit that operates in those who practice a lifestyle of sin. They have, by choice, become the enemy of God.

PART 3

God and Sinner

For You are not a God who takes pleasure in
wickedness, Nor shall evil dwell with You. The
boastful shall not stand in Your sight; You hate all
workers of iniquity. You shall destroy those who
speak falsehood; The Lord abhors the blood-
thirsty and deceitful man.

—Psalm 5:5 NKJV

In the beginning

The wrath of God, most certainly, is one of the most misunderstood
and distorted topics in the Bible. It is taught either as being done
away with by the cross of Jesus or that God will come down at ran-
dom to punish for the slightest offense. Neither approach is biblical!
God's wrath is always exact and deserved. It is not some burst of
emotional anger as we are predisposed to exhibit.

Ordinarily, people tend to shy away from talking about the
wrath of God due to its being so personal. All humans fall short of
perfection when they are compared with the holiness of God. And
today we respond just as Adam did in the garden when we have
to face God concerning our sin. The thought of God being angry
should cause us no little dread, but for some, it is really just an after-
thought. We tend to think greater of ourselves than we should as we

make excuses for our failure to meet God's standards. And just like Adam, we tend to shift blame and hide.

This sense of uneasiness that accompanies the matter is really our inbuilt fear of God and His judgment of our sin. It comes from the inward knowledge found within every human concerning God's wrath and dealings with sin (Romans 1:18–20). Sin is a personal issue and will be dealt with as such. Every man will come to terms with God concerning sin. There can be little doubt that we will be responsible for our actions just as Adam was. In his dealings with God, Adam not only placed the blame for his sin on Eve but also implied that God was ultimately responsible. He said that if God hadn't given Eve to him, he would never have done this independently. Refusing to accept responsibility for our actions is the same as Adam's failure.

After Adam disobeyed God, he was afraid to face the Creator. The reason being that the work of the tree of the knowledge of good and evil had activated Adam's conscience through his act of treason, and it condemned him. How difficult it must have been for Adam to know that he had to face God at some point! No doubt they expected God's visitation as usual. In their guilt, they tried to hide their sin by sewing fig leaves together. What a sense of loss and shame Adam must have sensed when faced with the knowledge that he had disobeyed the Father.

But despite their best efforts, they failed. How their conscience must have burned with guilt. Shame and fear were the instant results of Adam and Eve's first sin, which still continues in us today. Likewise, every person who has been born on this earth has this same knowledge of good and evil at work in them. We intuitively know that there comes a day that we will face God. Sin always causes a person to run and hide from God. Hiding alone is evidence of guilt. But hiding is not going to change the situation. It is impossible to hide from God (see Psalm 139:7–12; Jeremiah 23:24; Amos 9:2–3). David declared that God's presence would be there even if he made his bed in hell (see Psalm 139:8).

When Adam and Eve disobeyed God, many things changed. The most significant change was that death entered into their lives, both spiritually and physically. The intimate and personal fellowship with God no longer existed (see Colossians 1:20). They were no longer innocent and became sin conscious rather than God conscious. Shame and guilt caused them to hide from God because of their nakedness.

So who told Adam and Eve they were naked? There is no indication that Satan told Adam anything nor did God. This intuitive knowledge came from eating the fruit from the tree of the knowledge of good and evil. The conscience is the part of us that either accuses or excuses us (see Romans 2:15). Adam was not endowed with a sin conscience. He had no need of that because all he had knowledge of was good and perfect. This knowledge of sin came through experiencing the tree of the knowledge of good and evil.

Now because of Adam's actions (see Romans 3:23), we all have an active yet defective conscience. It may be that we can ignore its function or that it has been so seared with sin that it no longer works properly, but still, it is there. Its role is to condemn or confirm right from wrong in us (see Romans 2:15). I believe that when the enemy of God arrives at the throne of judgment, his conscience will once again speak. Thankfully, when the believer sins, we have the blood of Jesus to cleanse our consciences so that we can come into the presence of God without condemnation (see Hebrews 10:22). The enemy of God foolishly chooses to ignore the conviction of the conscience or that it no longer works properly. If we have a clear/clean conscience, then we can have confidence toward God. First John 3:21 states, "Beloved, if our heart condemn us not, then have we confidence toward God."

Before the fall, Adam only knew what God had given them, which was good. After disobeying God, they acquired the experiential knowledge of evil. Adam and Eve were not operating with a conscience that condemned them because they were without sin. So, the question remains, Were they more like God before or after the fall?

All who live in sin live with this guilt and fear even if it's in the far reaches of their mind. They may deny it, but still, it is at work. Additionally, some acknowledge the sin in their life and actually revel and rejoice in their ungodliness. They readily celebrate their sinfulness and mock God and the coming judgment. These are the enemies of God.

First Timothy 4:1–2 NKJV states, "Now the Spirit expressly says that in latter times some will depart from the faith, giving heed to deceiving spirits and doctrines of demons, speaking lies in hypocrisy, having their own conscience seared with a hot iron."

People with healthy consciences cannot consistently act contrary to their hearts; their consciences will convict them. Even those who have not been saved can listen and act upon their hearts leading. They can know right from wrong and can act accordingly. But people with "seared" consciences no longer feel that conviction; they have been deadened to sin. To say that something has been *seared with a hot iron* literally means "to a brand ['cauterize']" (*Strong's Concordance*). These are the enemies of God.

The word *seared* describes the effect of taking a hot iron and touching it to flesh to seal a wound and stop bleeding. In the process, the nerves are destroyed, and all sensory perception is lost. Similarly, sin can deaden people's consciences so that they are no longer convicted of sin. When this occurs, the enemy of God will always do what is right in their own eyes. Also, note that life experiences also can cause a deadening of sorts to the conscience. If we allow hurts and disappointments to linger, we can become insensitive to the wounds in others. We cease to feel the pain of others to protect ourselves from further injury. When we ignore the voice of conviction, our consciences become a little less sensitive, making it easier to repeat the offense and go further the next time. Eventually, it becomes as if we have no conscience; we sin without feeling any conviction. This is the dangerous state that all reprobates find themselves in. They continue to live ungodly lives, and after some time, God allows them to go their own way. Living in sin becomes natural to the enemy of God.

However arrogant and prideful the unrepentant may be, the judgment of God will be the same for everyone. Romans 2:16 NKJV states, "…in the day when God will judge the secrets of men by Jesus Christ, according to my gospel." Notice that God will judge "the secrets of men." No one gets by with anything. All men will be held accountable (see 1 Corinthians 4:5; Ecclesiastes 12:14; Luke 8:17, 12:1–4; Matthew 12:36; 1 Corinthians 3:13).

God is not like man

One problem that arises in thinking about God's wrath is that we are all too inclined to think of God in human terms. "You thought that I was just like you. I will reprove you and state the case in order before your eyes," God says in Psalm 50:21 NASB. "'My thoughts are not your thoughts, neither are your ways my ways,' saith the Lord. 'For as the heavens are higher than the earth, so are my ways higher than your ways, and my thoughts than your thoughts'" (Isaiah 55:8–9). He is perfect in all His ways. He is always in control. He is not motivated as we are through the works of the flesh. D. A. Carson describes the Father in this way:

> [25]All of God's emotions, including His love in all its aspects, cannot be divorced from God's knowledge, God's power, God's will. If God loves, it is because He chooses to love; if He suffers, it is because He chooses to suffer. God is impassible in the sense that He sustains no "passion," no emotion, that makes Him vulnerable from the outside, over which He has no control, or which He has not foreseen.

Dr. Carson writes further, saying, "The price of diluting God's wrath is diminishing God's holiness."

Unlike the emotions of man, God's feelings never waver and never change. He is not moved out of fleshly passions or by circumstances as we are. That alone makes it absolutely unlike any human feeling we have ever experienced.

God's love

Let's consider how the Bible defines the love of God. Agape love, which is the love of God, involves faithfulness, commitment, and an act of the will. Agape love is beautifully described in 1 Corinthians 13. Interestingly, human love and divine love have some of the same characteristics and are based on a decision rather than an emotion and distinguished from the other types of love by their selfless nature and strong character.

Agape can also be defined as charity or the giving of aid to those without. This is a good definition, but it doesn't encompass all of what *agape* is about. *Agape* love is indifferent to the needs of self but for the greatest good of another. It is not born out of emotions or feelings but from will and choice. *Agape* requires faithfulness, commitment, and sacrifice without expecting anything in return. Agape love is made known by what it does, not just how it feels. God's love can be seen most clearly at the cross because while we were yet sinners, Christ died for us. His compassion for mankind is based upon His will and His decision to do so. He loves us only because He is compassionate and full of mercy, not because we are loveable. God is under no obligation to anyone for anything. He loves because that is who He is. He answers to no one, nor is He required to give any account for His decisions. God has no obligation to sinful men except to condemn. His sovereignty in all things allows God to show mercy to whom He desires. He offered no mercy to the angels when they sinned, even though it was His prerogative was to do so. "I will have mercy on whom I will have mercy" (Romans 9:18). Therefore, the love of God comes strictly out of His decision to do so.

God delights far more in His mercy than in His wrath. However, His compassion and mercy must be viewed against the backdrop of His anger toward sin and the sinner. Because of His mercy and compassion for mankind, one can see that His wrath was poured out upon Jesus. Wrath and mercy are connected eternally through the cross of Jesus. Because of His holiness, sin must be confronted, and the price must be paid in full. If our sin is not accounted for, then the holiness of God must come into question. Jesus is God's greatest example of His love against His wrath.

God's love is the highest form of love in the Bible. It is a perfect and unconditional type of love that surpasses circumstances because the love of God is not based on emotions. If His love was dependent upon our loving Him, then it would be no better than how we, as humans, love. He loves us because of His infallible nature. God's love can never conflict with His holiness, so therefore, sin cannot be tolerated. God's love is perfect, and so is His wrath. No quality about Him is less excellent than another.

We cannot perceive anything as He does; we cannot understand the love and mercy of God in Christ Jesus. He is beyond our finite comprehension because He is infinite. Even the greatest scientific minds of our time have failed to grasp the awesomeness of the Lord. A. W. Pink had this description of God:

> [26]He is solitary in his majesty, unique in His excellency, peerless in his perfections. He sustains all, but is Himself independent of all. He gives to all, but is enriched by none. Such a God cannot be found out by searching. He can be known only as he is revealed to the heart by the Holy Spirit through the Word.

We must allow Scripture, not human experience, to shape our understanding of God's emotions and feelings. Those who study the subject of wrath through the lens of Scripture will soon discover that God's anger and love are on a totally different level than human passions. Suffice it to say that God's divine affections will always remain hidden as a mystery for the most part. His emotions are to stay as an impenetrable, profound mystery, far above our understanding.

God is holy

The word *holy* (hallowed, holiest, holiness) appears over six hundred times in the Bible, yet no man can grasp what God is truly like. The term *holy* is mentioned 431 times in the Old Testament (not counting the word *holiness*). I think we should be concerned with holiness if we intend to enter the kingdom of heaven. Matthew Henry was quoted saying, "No attribute of God is more dreadful to sinners than his holiness."

First Samuel 2:2 NKJV states, "No one is holy like the LORD, For there is none besides You, Nor is there any rock like our God."

The most defining characteristic of God is His unspeakable holiness. The holiness of God describes both His goodness and His power. It is a totally separate, superior, and unequaled power. In fact, God's righteousness is so overwhelming that no being can approach Him without the blood of Christ. Because God is a holy God, a Savior was necessary before a man could ever approach His throne. God knows that human beings can never meet His standards of perfect holiness. So in order for man to get back to God, there had to be a spotless, sinless sacrifice to pay the debt for humanity's sins. God sent Jesus as a way to transfer holiness to sinful men and women.

Everything about God is pure, undefiled, and righteous. His holiness is the very essence of who He is, and it is through His holiness that He can judge aright. You can't separate His love from His wrath, as they are both equally pure. His being holy refers to His disconnectedness from sin and sinner, His otherworldliness cannot be described. Holiness is His divine existence and indicates His complete and immeasurable faultlessness. Man has lost the fear of God over time because we have made idols in our own hearts that love us enough not to judge our sin. However comforting that may be, this is not the God of creation.

Jeremiah 17:9–10 NKJV states, "The heart is deceitful above all things, And desperately wicked; Who can know it? I, the LORD, search the heart, I test the mind, Even to give every man according to his ways, According to the fruit of his doings."

The enemy of God does not consider the holiness of our God. He doesn't view himself the same way as God does. If ever God's enemy could see himself in the view that God takes, he would cry out as the Prophet Isaiah when he saw the Lord.

Isaiah 6:5 NKJV states, "So I said: 'Woe is me, for I am undone! Because I am a man of unclean lips, And I dwell in the midst of a people of unclean lips; For my eyes have seen the King, The LORD of hosts.'"

Because of our inflated view of ourselves, we learn to tolerate unholiness in our lives as well as the lives of others. Some have come to believe that living in sin is simply a natural and expected way of life. The enemy of God is totally indifferent to God's holiness. He may fear God's power and admire His wisdom to some degree, but holiness is not even in his thoughts. If God's holiness and absolute power were revealed to the rebellious, they would quickly see their predicament and repent.

Being the perfect Uncreated One, God does not conform to any other standard of holiness because He alone is the standard. God is holy with an immeasurable and impenetrable fullness of purity. Because He is holy, all His characteristics are incapable of being anything other than what they are. He is unchangeable in all of His attributes.

Old and New Testament

As we study further, we find that God's wrath can be found in the Old Testament and the New Testament. A. W. Pink comments, [27]"A study of the concordance will show that there are more references in Scripture to the anger, fury, and wrath of God, than there are to His love and tenderness." In Genesis 22:16, God says, "By myself have I sworn." In Psalm 89:35, he declares, "Once have I sworn by my holiness." While in Psalm 95:11, he affirms, "I swear in my wrath." We can see by these scriptures his "wrath" is equal to his "holiness"; He swears by the one as much as by the other!

If we teach that God loves the sinner and hates the sin without bringing the balance of truth, people tend to think flippantly about sin. Their attitude will be as follows: "I'm not that bad!" or "God loves me regardless of how I live" or "He will overlook my sin," or even worse, "God knows that I'm a sinner!" But sin is so grave to God that He sent His Son Jesus to the cross as our substitute to take upon

Himself God's wrath. Without Christ, every sinner must pay for the sin of rejecting Christ. I believe that the first thought that may go through minds of those in hell is, "I didn't have to be here!"

Because we are in the time of grace, sinners tend to take advantage of His patience. God's death sentence remains upon all sinners who are not truly born again. John 3:18 NKJV states, "He who believes in Him is not condemned, but he who does not believe is condemned already because he has not believed in the name of the only begotten Son of God."

Again! John 3:36 NKJV states, "He who believes in the Son has everlasting life; and he who does not believe the Son shall not see life, but the wrath of God abides on him."

A future time is coming for mankind when God will pour out His wrath on all the earth (see Revelation 6:17, 11:18, 14:19, 15:1, 7, 16:1, 19, 19:15). Jesus has come not to condemn people in this present age but to bring them grace and truth (John 1:14, 3:17). Because judgment has been delayed does not in any way mean that it isn't coming. The enemy of God fails to consider this and lives his life as he sees fit.

According to the Word of God, the enemy of God is presently under the Old Testament law's wrath (see John 5:45; Romans 4:15; Galatians 3:10; John 3:18). Therefore, unless they repent, they will suffer the wrath of God eternally (see Romans 2:6–9; Revelation 20:13–15). Not only are we saved from the wrath to come (Matthew 3:7; 1 Thessalonians 5:9; Revelation 6:17, 11:18) but also from the present wrath, that is, the curse of the Old Testament law (Galatians 3:13). People are often deceived into believing that God no longer has wrath or punishment for the unbeliever. This is a lie! Our heavenly Father certainly is kind, merciful, and patient; but He is also a God of judgment and will punish all who remains as His enemy.

So what makes the modern-day preacher seem so hard-pressed to talk about God's wrath? If the Bible describes God's wrath in such vivid terms of anger, shouldn't it be okay if we do the same using the same approach and language? I certainly do not condone abusing anyone with harshness, but we must speak the truth in love. We are no different than Adam when he sinned. We still want to hide and transfer blame for our failure. It must be noted that fear is the first negative emotion exhibited after the fall. Fear results from not trusting in God and His perfect love (see 1 John 4:18). Fear comes because we know in our hearts that the flawless and exact judgment of God will come to us all. It can't be denied, only ignored.

The word *sin,* found in Romans 6:6 (KJV), is not the individual acts of sin but instead of the sin nature or "old man" itself. It's something we are born with, and without Christ, we are held liable to God for those sins. Those who do not receive the new birth (see John 3:3) are currently held liable for not accepting Jesus (see Mark 3:29). However, those who choose to receive the new birth through faith in Jesus no longer have a sinful nature (see Romans 6:6) and will not be accountable for this death payment. Because of sin, somebody has to die! That someone was Jesus!

Author Jerry Bridges wrote, [28]"God does not exalt His mercy at the expense of His justice. And to maintain His justice, all sin without exception must be punished." It is daunting indeed to realize that God's judgment will be absolutely accurate and earned by every individual who has ever lived. This wrath is not some uncalculated emotional pouring out of anger toward someone who has offended Him. Instead, it will be the price for offending His holiness. It is a reckoning with the Creator. God's wrath does not contain the sinful emotions associated with human anger. But it does have a fierce intensity arising from His opposition to sin and His determination to punish it to the utmost, as it is His right to do so. What's more, His final judgment toward sin and sinner will last for all eternity. Thankfully, His mercy and compassion caused His dying for us so that he might make us into the apple of his eye.

God hates the sin and the sinner

The statement *God hates the sin but loves the sinner* has become the philosophy of American evangelism today. The origin of this thought comes from a statement made by Ghandi. While the intent is meant for the good and there may be a bit of truth in context, the statement is inaccurate. It should be abandoned because it portrays an easy believism and says that there is no need for repentance. In effect, it diminishes God's holiness. We can't call God a good God if He didn't address the issue of sin. He is a god of perfect justice; therefore, He must be a god of flawless judgment because the two are inseparable. The scriptures clearly show that God loves justice. He is quick to show mercy to sinners while hating them in their sin. Why? Because of His holiness, God is a lover of righteousness and justice. His righteousness is a reflection of His nature. When we do what is right, we are acting correctly and mirroring God's own nature. When we sin, we are actually insulting God. Sin is offensive to our Holy Father, and the payment or penalty for our sin is death. Thankfully, Jesus took the penalty for us out of His compassion and mercy.

When we reject His offering of Jesus, then we choose to abide under the wrath of God (see John 3:36, 5:24). God's own righteousness is offered as a gift to sinners who accept Jesus Christ as their Savior. According to His grace and mercy, this gift is given in response to our faith (Romans 3:23–26; Ephesians 2:3–7). His mercy and grace is not given in spite of His justice but because He has compassion toward the sinner. If He didn't offer a means of escape, God would violate His own character of being righteous. He loved us so much that even though our sin demands our death, He sent His Son to be our substitute upon the cross. By this, His love was demonstrated, and His justice was not violated. The death of Jesus satisfied God's requirement for justice (1 Thessalonians 1:10, 5:9). Conversely, He hates sin and the sinner with the same fury and intensity because sin goes against His holy nature.

Understanding love

Universalism is a philosophy that teaches the thought that God loves everyone and that everyone is redeemed. But the concept cannot be found anywhere in the Bible. Clearly, God hates sinners, but He also has mercy on them out of compassion and offers salvation. The Scriptures tell us of His mercy in Romans 9:15: "God will have mercy on who He will have mercy and compassion on who He will have compassion." The critical difference between love and compassion is that love is a deep feeling of fondness and attachment toward someone. On the other hand, compassion is a sympathetic pity and concern for others' sufferings or misfortunes. When you are compassionate, you will desire to ease another's suffering even if you don't like them.

> Who is a God like You, pardoning iniquity and passing over the transgression of the remnant of His heritage? He does not retain His anger forever, because He delights in mercy. He will again have compassion on us and will subdue our iniquities. You will cast all our sins into the depths of the sea. (Micah 7:18–19)

God's righteous hatred is so different from our definition and experiences. We must see the application through the eyes of God according to the scriptures. Sadly, Christianity has often misused the terms love and hate to somehow lessen the blow of conviction to the offender's conscience, which is the last thing the unrepentant needs. However religious it may sound, again, it was Gandhi who said, "[29]I like your Christ, but I do not like your Christians because they look nothing like your Christ…"

The enemy of God often teaches John 3:16 to show that "God loves the sinner but hates the sin" to justify their sin. But the verse does not say that God loves sinners; it says He loves the world. So, the question begs. What world does God love? He loves the world He originally created and declared as good—not this present fallen world. That is not to say that He doesn't show great compassion to the inhabitants because certainly He does. We can see in the scriptures that His mercy alone is what keeps us from hell.

> And I said, "My strength and my hope Have perished from the LORD." Remember my affliction and roaming, The wormwood and the gall. My soul still remembers And sinks within me. This I recall to my mind, Therefore I have hope.

Through the LORD'S mercies we are not con-
sumed, Because His compassions fail not. They
are new every morning; Great is Your faithfulness. (Lamentations 3:18–23 NKJV)

Not many ever question the existence or the reality of hell. It is
a place of unthinkable eternal torment. Those who reject Christ will
spend eternity there but not because God diminished His mercy. It
was His love at the beginning that gave us the gift of free will. We
can accept Him and receive love, or we can reject Him and receive
wrath. God, out of His immeasurable mercy, is giving us the choice
of accepting Him or rejecting Him. Those in hell have simply chosen
to reject God and His mercy, and He has simply enforced their will.
God's mercy means that even though we deserve punishment, we do
not receive it. He asserts His compassion for us so that we can avoid
a just condemnation.

Adam's choice

Genesis 3 teaches us about the fall of Adam because of his
choice to disobey. It also teaches that all creation fell with him. The
world that God had created as good was now cursed because of man's
sin. Therefore, both man and the world (i.e., the fallen world) were
no longer good but cursed. God, with a broken heart, repented that
had He created man and the earth! While God does not change in
His attributes, we can understand that His repentance presents a
truth about God. In His consistency with His immutability, He has
a changed position in respect to a changed man.

Genesis 6:5–8 states, "The Lord saw the wickedness of man was
great in the earth, every intention of the thoughts of his heart was
only evil continually. And the Lord was sorry that He had made man
on the earth and it grieved Him to His heart."

What an indictment upon mankind to know that God cre-
ated such perfection but was grieved by His own creation. The New
International Version says, "His heart was filled with pain." The
Living Bible says, "It broke his heart." So the Lord in His grief said,

"I will blot out man whom I have created from the face of the land, man and animals and creeping things and birds of the heavens, for I am sorry that I made them." But Noah found favor in the eyes of the Lord. The Lord had compassion and grace for Noah, but had Noah refused to obey God, he would have suffered the same fate as the others who didn't believe.

The Scriptures are clear

We can never find in Scripture where God's standard of holiness has changed (God can definitely change His mind but never His character). He is holy and perfect in both wrath and love. His judgments are absolute and true. To say that God's love is totally unconditional is to say that we can come to God and live as we desire without repentance or penalty for sin. There are requirements that must be followed. The requirements for His mercy are that we repent and follow Him.

It must be understood that God's wrath is not rendered toward us as merciless blind anger. He never acts out of raw emotion as we usually do but out of His holiness. His holiness demands that sin must be dealt with. Because we are sinful by nature, His fury will be exact and entirely deserved by those who reject His redemption plan. While the ferocity of His wrath is not displayed yet, the unbelieving can be sure that it is coming.

Yes! A time is coming when God will pour out His wrath on all the earth (see Revelation 6:17, 14:19, 15:1, 19:15) today. Those who do not believe in Jesus as Lord and Savior remain under the Old Testament law's wrath (see John 5:45; Romans 4:15; Galatians 3:10; John 3:18). Unless enemies of God repent, they will suffer God's wrath eternally (see Romans 2:6–9; Revelation 20:13–15).

Can it really be true that God hates the sinner? What do the Scriptures say about God hating the sinner? Read these scriptures and ask the Holy Spirit to speak to your heart.

He who believes in the Son has everlasting life,
and he who does not believe the Son shall not see

life, but the wrath of God abides on him. (John 3:36 NKJV)

For You are not a God who takes pleasure in wickedness, Nor shall evil dwell with You. The boastful shall not stand in Your sight; You hate all workers of iniquity. You shall destroy those who speak falsehood; The LORD abhors the blood-thirsty and deceitful man. (Psalm 5:4–6 NKJV)

The LORD tests the righteous, But the wicked and the one who loves violence His soul hates. Upon the wicked He will rain coals; Fire and brimstone and a burning wind Shall be the por-tion of their cup. (Psalm 11:5–6 NKJV)

I have forsaken My house, I have left My heri-tage; I have given the dearly beloved of My soul into the hand of her enemies. My heritage is to Me like a lion in the forest; It cries out against Me; Therefore I have hated it. (Jeremiah 12:7–8 NKJV)

"All their wickedness is in Gilgal, For there I hated them. Because of the evil of their deeds I will drive them from My house; I will love them no more. All their princes are rebellious. Ephraim is stricken, Their root is dried up; They shall bear no fruit. Yes, were they to bear children, I would kill the darlings of their womb." My God will cast them away, Because they did not obey Him; And they shall be wanderers among the nations. (Hosea 9:15–17 NKJV)

If we understand the word *hate* used in the Bible, the term must be defined in context. In the Hebrew language, hate means "to hate;

scorn; an enemy to be ejected from one's territory; enemies; enemy; foes; hateful; being set against; opposed; detested; despised; and with which one wishes to have no contact or relationship. It is therefore the opposite of love. Whereas love draws and unites, hate separates and keeps distant. The hated and hating persons are considered foes or enemies and are considered vile, deplorable, and utterly unappealing." With these definitions in view, how can we define hate in any other way? Other dictionaries show hatred to be just as it really is. "To dislike greatly; to have a great aversion to."

The Prophet Isaiah vividly describes how God despises and loathes the sinner.

> From the sole of the foot even to the head, There is no soundness in it, But wounds and bruises and putrefying sores; They have not been closed or bound up, Or soothed with ointment. (Isaiah 1:6 NKJV)

The Psalms makes it clear how God views the sinner.

> For You are not a God who takes pleasure in wickedness, Nor shall evil dwell with You. The boastful shall not stand in Your sight; You hate all workers of iniquity. You shall destroy those who speak falsehood; The LORD abhors the bloodthirsty and deceitful man. (Psalm 5:4–6 NKJV)

> The wicked plots against the just, And gnashes at him with his teeth. The Lord laughs at him, For He sees that his day is coming. (Psalm 37:12–13 NKJV)

It often seems that the wicked people prosper beyond what the child of God may, but we must remember that the Lord has an eternal view unlike our own. He sees the end of the wicked. It's only by the mercy of the Lord that the wicked prosper for a brief moment, but payday is certain. Psalm 36:1–4 speaks of the evil and how they are self-deceived (see Psalm 36:2) into thinking they will not be held accountable for their actions. People flatter or deceive themselves into believing they will not be caught or even worse, not caring if they do get caught. The enemies of God will always act and speak in ungodly ways and give themselves over to doing evil, not counting the cost. The old proverb holds true in that "there is no one so blind as the one who refuses to see." The enemy of God is walking in self-imposed blindness that will require a very high price on the day of judgment. Please consider the attitude of the Lord concerning His enemies.

> But the wicked shall perish; And the enemies of the LORD, Like the splendor of the meadows, shall vanish. Into smoke they shall vanish away. (Psalm 37:20 NKJV)

> He who justifies the wicked, and he who condemns the just, Both of them alike are an abomination to the LORD. (Proverbs 17:15 NKJV)

These verses alone do not lend themselves well to the notion that God loves the sinner. God is impartial in His judgments; His hatred of sin also includes the sinner.

> The LORD tests the righteous, But the wicked and the one who loves violence His soul hates. Upon the wicked He will rain coals; Fire and brimstone and a burning wind Shall be the portion of their cup. (Psalm 11:5–6 NKJV)

> For You are not a God who delights in wickedness; evil may not dwell with You. The boastful shall not stand before Your eyes; You hate all evil doers. (Psalm 5:4–5)

These scriptures show God has a hatred for evildoers or—in other words—sinners! How many are included in the word *all* in Psalm 5:4–5? Thankfully, God has an abundance of mercy and compassion for the sinner because of His love nature. The Scripture (see Matthew 5:45) says God pours rain on the just and unjust; He does this because of His mercy and compassion! God can have pity on sinners without loving them as such. The false teaching of universalism says that God loves everyone and that everyone is redeemed, but this is far from accurate! The Word of God shows just the opposite. Still, He has great mercy and offers salvation to anyone who will repent and receive God's forgiveness through Jesus. The cross of Jesus, for example, is the perfect instance of that love. His endurance and patience with the unrepented are other examples of the love of God.

The mercy of God toward His enemies

God is a god of great mercy as well as exacting justice, and he has declared that He will "by no means clear the guilty" (see Exodus 34:7). The Lord is merciful, gracious, and long-suffering but is not forever suffering. His holiness demands that justice be served. He may defer His judgment, but it will come. There will be no judgment except to receive rewards for those who have accepted Jesus's payment for sin (see 1 Corinthians 3:12–15). Jesus drew all of God's wrath to Himself, and that in itself is the most significant expression of the mercy of God (see John 12:32). Just think about the idea of God not ever extending His mercy except for your keeping the law. Consider the thought that if the Holy Ghost had not come to you, you would have no chance at redemption. Our Father is not obligated to receive us other than by faith in Jesus. But for the ungodly, who refuse to receive Jesus as their Savior, a day of reckoning is coming that will extract full payment for rejecting Christ. Romans 5:8 NKJV states, "But God demonstrates His own love toward us, in that while we were still sinners, Christ died for us." This verse is commonly quoted to illustrate God's unconditional love toward sinners, and it is true. But in context, we can see that we were saved from His holy wrath even though we were sinners and undeserving of such mercy.

Romans 5:9–10 NKJV states, "Much more then, having now been justified by His blood, we shall be saved from wrath through Him. For if when we were enemies we were reconciled to God through the death of His Son, much more, having been reconciled, we shall be saved by His life."

Thankfully, God has shown His benevolence toward the sinner and compassion to them and wills their good. So, in context, there is some truth in the fact that God loves all men unconditionally, both sinners and saints. That is not at all contrary to the teaching of God's hatred. His mercy is such that He never wishes for men to perish (see 2 Peter 3:9). His disposition toward man is to show mercy. He is long-suffering, and He is slow to wrath and quick to forgive. Psalm 103:8 NKJV states, "The LORD is merciful and gracious, Slow to anger, and abounding in mercy." He does not send quick judgment when we sin but convicts us by His Spirit and gives us time to consider our ways. Many verses show God's love toward the man as found in the example of Jesus's death on the cross (see John 3:16; Romans 5:8; 1 John 3:16). This type of mercy for man is unconditional.

Romans 9:15 tells us that God will have mercy on whomever He desires. Note that love is not used in this Scripture because mercy and love are different. A person can have mercy and compassion toward those whom they do not care for. Those born again are saved because He is a god of mercy and "delights in mercy."

> Who is a God like You, pardoning iniquity and passing over the transgression of the remnant of His heritage? He does not retain His anger forever, because He delights in mercy. He will again have compassion on us, and will subdue our iniquities. You will cast all our sins into the depths of the sea. (Micah 7:18–19)

It is hard to comprehend how God hates and loves unrepentant sinners simultaneously and with the same intensity. Whenever Scripture speaks of God hating the sinner, it is by no means the same kind of hate we express toward one another. His nature is love (see 1 John 4:8), but He is also righteous (see Psalm 7:9) and holy (see Isaiah 6:3). The very fact that He does not destroy all humanity for its sin against Him is an excellent example of His love.

It must be understood that God's wrath against sinners is not an emotional outburst of anger. It is, however, an entirely rational and willed response to sin against His holiness. At the same time, His mercy was extended to His enemies. He does not accept sinners just the way they are; they are required to repent (change of heart) and accept Jesus as Lord and follow Him to be accepted (see Acts 10:35). Even the most hardened heart can indeed come to Him and receive forgiveness, but He doesn't love sinners outside of the terms He gives us. He does not provide them unconditional approval, unconditional acceptance, total forgiveness, or unconditional friendship without repentance (see Luke 13:3-5).

Thus, with God being who He is, there is nothing impossible or wrong concerning His wrath and love being directed toward the same individual or people at once. In other words, He hates all sinners in a perfectly holy way and still lovingly forgives the sinner (see Malachi 1:3; Revelation 2:6; 2 Peter 3:9). As humans, we fail to love with perfect love, nor can we hate with a righteous hatred because we still struggle with our fleshly emotions. But God can both love and hate with equal intensity because He is God. Again, because He is God, He can love us with the same resolve to save us even while He hates us. His thoughts are not like ours.

Psalm 50:21 NKJV states, "These things you have done, and I kept silent; You thought that I was altogether like you, But I will rebuke you, And set them in order before your eyes." Other scriptures teach the same thing concerning our thoughts and the thoughts of God.

Isaiah 55:8–9 NKJV states, "'For My thoughts are not your thoughts, Nor are your ways My ways,' says the LORD. 'For as the heavens are higher than the earth, So are My ways higher than your ways, And My thoughts than your thoughts.'"

The tension that these scriptures pose generates many difficult questions. How do we really understand God? Have we made Him into something of our own imaginations and assumptions? How can God both hate and love the same person in the same way? Suppose you find this concept of God uncomfortable with your idea about who God really is. Maybe we are not as familiar with God as we once believed.

It's essential to have the Word's whole counsel to understand the nature of our God as far as we are able. Because of who He is, we can never fully comprehend Him, but we have the written Word that has revealed some attributes that can help us know what we need to know. Our trouble comes with an imbalance of the truth that can cause the pendulum of doctrinal belief to swing wildly in either direction. On the one hand, many Christians are so used to hearing only about God's grace and love that any mention of wrath is offensive. This is unfortunate because not speaking about His anger toward sin and sinner actually diminishes the power of God's forgiveness.

To understand the heart of God in as much as been revealed, we should hold fast to God's whole counsel, not just certain parts that are pleasant to our ears. God's wrath is as much a part of God as the love of God revealed in Jesus Christ. Let us be careful and diligent not to water down the truth found in the scriptures in these last days. Paul told the Ephesians he did not hold back anything profitable from them but had declared God's whole counsel (see Acts 20:20).

Second Timothy 3:16–17 NKJV states, "All Scripture is given by inspiration of God, and is profitable for doctrine, for reproof, for correction, for instruction in righteousness, that the man of God may be complete, thoroughly equipped for every good work."

To His enemies, God may be a simple private interpretation of the scriptures or a college intellectual's suggestion that there may be an unknown entity's slight possibility. While they might even go so far as to positively affirm the likelihood of a god, the likelihood that one can actually prove it remains small and unknown to the individual. He remains as an idea or, at best, merely a theory. However, the Bible has revealed God as being a holy God.

Clearly, the topic of God's wrath can be seen through the Holy Scriptures.

> For the wrath of God is revealed from heaven
> against all ungodliness and unrighteousness of
> men, who suppress the truth in unrighteous-
> ness, because what may be known of God is
> manifest in them, for God has shown it to them.
> For since the creation of the world His invisible
> attributes are clearly seen, being understood by
> the things that are made, even His eternal power
> and Godhead, so that they are without excuse.
> (Romans 1:18–20 NKJV)

Additionally, many of the first fifty psalms tell us about God hating the sinner and not just the sin (see Romans 1:18–23; John 3:36).

Society and religion have made a god that is more palatable than Jehovah. The god erected by mankind fails to confront sin, nor does anyone tremble and fear because of any judgment. What this false god accepts or rejects is dependent on the individual. Just as an idol made by man, it will stand silent against sin. As man has tried to cover up his iniquity, his god moves further from the truth. God's wrath has been revealed to every person's heart; there will be no excuse for those who chose to ignore this inner witness. We are without excuse. A tremendous accounting will be when people stand before God and answer for the sin in their lives. There will be no excuse because, in their hearts, they knew differently. The fact that people ignore that revelation doesn't void the fact that God has placed it there.

If the Bible describes God's wrath in such vivid terms of anger, we would do well if we were to follow Gods thoughts and language. I believe the problem we have in talking about judgment is that God's perfect and exact judgment will come to all who don't believe. This judgment will be accurate and absolutely earned by the individual. God, because He is holy, cannot tolerate the assault on His divine majesty by a rebel. The wrath of God is not some uncalculated emotion toward someone who has offended Him but rather the price for offending His holiness. It is the necessary response of God. Furthermore, God's wrath is not motivated by the sinful emotions associated with human anger. *It does, however,* have a fierce intensity arising from His firm opposition to sin and His determination to punish it to the utmost, as it is His right to do so.

God finds mankind inexcusably wicked and rebellious. We were made in His image, yet we rebelled against Him.

Another problem that arises about God's wrath is that we are all too inclined to think of God's emotions in human terms. "You thought that I was just like you. I will reprove you and state the case in order before your eyes," God says in Psalm 50:21 NASB. "'My thoughts are not your thoughts, neither are your ways my ways,' saith the Lord. 'And, For as the heavens are higher than the earth, so are my ways higher than your ways, and my thoughts than your thoughts'" (Isaiah 55:8–9). Again the Scripture reminds us that the affections of God are ultimately impenetrable (see Ephesians 3:19; Romans 11:33). And that His ways are perfect. He is always in control and is not motivated as we are through our flesh.

Notice, however, that not one aspect of love in the Bible has anything to do with our feelings.

Through the lens of Scripture, those who study the matter will soon discover that God's Word places God's wrath and love on a totally different level than human passions. Suffice it to say that God's divine affections will always remain hidden as a mystery for the most part. His emotions will always stay as an impenetrable, profound mystery. Far above our understanding, God burns with holiness, and no man can grasp what God is truly like. The word *holy* (hallowed, holiest, holiness) appears over six hundred times in the Bible. The term *holy* is mentioned times in the Old Testament (not counting the word *holiness*). I think we should be concerned with holiness if we intend to enter the kingdom of heaven.

Holy is the Lord

The Hebrew definition of holy is *qodesh*, which means "apartness," "sacredness," or "separateness," showing that He is altogether holy, sacred, set apart, and separate from His creation. The idea is that God is the most disconnected of all beings but is not aloof and cold toward us. Traditional religion teaches that God is *impassible*—

not knowing about suffering, pain, or the ebb and flow of involuntary passions. In the words of the *Westminster Confession of Faith*, God is "without body, parts, or *passions*, immutable." Does God not have any emotion or passion? Can He be grieved or pleased? Can the God of the Bible be touched with our feelings?

Consider for a moment the thought of a god without passions. Is this a god that can relate to our daily needs? Please read Genesis 5:6–7: "*God saw that the wickedness of man was great in the earth, and that every imagination of the thoughts of his heart was only evil continually. And it repented the Lord that he had made man on the earth, and it grieved him at his heart*" (emphasis added). In fact, Scripture frequently ascribes different displays of emotions from God. From scriptures, we can see that God can be grieved (Psalm 78:40), angry (Deuteronomy 1:37), pleased (1 Kings 3:10), joyful (Zephaniah 3:17), and moved by pity (Judges 2:18). There are New Testament examples of God having and displaying emotions. The Father was pleased with the Son (Matthew 3:17), Jesus was grieved (Mark 3:5), and faith pleases the Father (Hebrews 11:6). To say that God has no emotions or is impassionate also takes away God's divine love for His children.

God is eternal, transcendent, and holy, not given to passions and thought processes as we are. His view is immortal, and He can see time from the beginning to its end in one view. Not even angels are like Him! The heavenly creatures found flying around His eternal throne continue to cry, "Holy, holy, holy." Isaiah 6:2–3 NKJV states, "Above it stood seraphim; each one had six wings: with two he covered his face, with two he covered his feet, and with two he flew. And one cried to another and said: 'Holy, holy, holy is the LORD of hosts; The whole earth is full of His glory!'" He is separate from all else.

The theology that does away with God's wrath results in a gospel that makes light of sin, which takes away any fear of God or His punishment. Having no fear causes people to think lightly about their real spiritual corruption. They say, "It is okay to sin" or "God loves me just as I am and will just overlook my sin." However, Malachi 3:6 tells us that God changes not. He is immutable. If God never changes, then neither does his hatred for sin. By this, we can conclude that no part of His standards of holiness has changed as well. Claiming ignorance will in no way excuse man for not knowing about God's wrath. Do you know why? Romans 2:15 KJV states, "Which shew the work of the law written in their hearts, their conscience also bearing witness, and their thoughts the mean while accusing or else excusing one another."

Many fail to see God as a consuming fire of holiness that judges sin. [30]D. A. Carson once explained it this way:

> The reason is that in itself, wrath, unlike love, is not one of the intrinsic perfections of God. Rather, it is a function of God's holiness against sin. Where there is no sin, there is no wrath, but there will always be love in God. Where God in His holiness confronts His image-bearers in their rebellion, there must be wrath. Otherwise, God is not the jealous God He claims to be, and His holiness is questioned. The price of diluting God's wrath is diminishing God's holiness.

Through our limited human intellect, it is impossible to correctly comprehend His divine holiness. It stands apart and is exclusive, unapproachable, incomprehensible, and unattainable. One may fear God's power and admire His wisdom, but His holiness and righteousness cannot even be imagined. When John the Revelator saw Jesus for the first time in heaven, he fell as a dead man because of the power in Jesus's holiness. Because He is holy, His attributes are utterly divine, which includes His love and His wrath.

Revelation 1:17 NKJV states, "And when I saw Him, I fell at His feet as dead. But He laid His right hand on me, saying to me, 'Do not be afraid; I am the First and the Last.'"

The New Testament word used for holy or holiness is the Greek word *hagios*. It means "pure, morally blameless" or "set apart" for sacred use. The term *holy* is found in the New Testament 180 times, not to mention the word *holiness*. Clearly, holiness is vital to God, and He commands His followers to be as He is. This command may seem to be unattainable in our physical and soulish part, but we are to strive toward this goal. Thankfully, we are as holy as Jesus in our born-again spirits (see Ephesians 4:24) because the Father places holiness in our spirit man when we accept Christ (see 2 Corinthians 5:21). And because of Jesus we are able to live holy and acceptable to the Father.

First Peter 1:15–16 KJV states, "But as he which hath called you is holy, so be ye holy in all manner of conversation; Because it is written, Be ye holy; for I am holy."

The ways of God are not our ways, and His thoughts are not our thoughts (see Isaiah 55:8). But we can't deny that God hates the sinner along with his sin, and His wrath is upon anyone who opposes Him.

James 4:4 KJV states, "Ye adulterers and adulteresses, know ye not that the friendship of the world is enmity with God? whosoever, therefore will be a friend of the world is the enemy of God."

This is a powerful scripture that reveals how the Lord views friendship with the world. To God, it is considered adultery. He hates it. It's consorting with the enemy. Those who cross the lines to fellowship with God's enemy will find themselves at odds with God. So the question begs, What does friendship with the world entail? According to 1 John 2:15–16, it involves the lust of the flesh, the lust of the eyes, and life's pride. Romans 8:7 shows that the carnal mind is enmity against God. That is to say, we are the enemies of God because of our unrenewed minds.

Further, God hates His enemies with righteous, perfected hate, unlike man's self-centered, emotionally charged hatred. God is love, holy, and righteous. Having these characteristics, God cannot even look upon sinners as He could not look upon His Son on the cross.

Matthew 27:46 ASV states, "And about the ninth hour Jesus cried with a loud voice, saying, 'Eli, Eli, lama sabachthani? that is, My God, my God, why hast thou forsaken me?'"

To imply that God loves the sinner *and* hates the sin is an affront to His holiness, and the thought cannot be found in the Bible. "You are not a God who delights in wickedness; evil may not dwell with you. The boastful shall not stand before your eyes; you hate all evildoers" (Psalm 5:4–5). Or "The Lord tests the righteous, but his soul hates the wicked and the one who loves violence" (Psalm 11:5). Many scriptures show that the wrath of God rests on both sin (see Romans 1:18–23) and the sinner (see Romans 1:24–32, 2:5; John 3:36). How can we separate the sin from the sinner as they are not exclusive to each other?

God can hate sinners in all holiness while also having compassion for sinners and desiring them to repent and receive forgiveness (see Psalm 5, 11; Malachi 1:3; Revelation 2:6; 2 Peter 3:9). As human beings, we cannot love nor hate as He does. We cannot love with a perfect love because of our sin-flawed emotions, nor can we hate with a perfect hatred for the same reason. God can love and hate with holy righteousness in His perfection because He is a holy and sinless God, and He hates without evil intent. He hates the sinner in a perfectly holy way and still forgives the sinner (see Malachi 1:3; Corinthians 5:19; Revelation 2:6; 2 Peter 3:9). It is only because of His immeasurable mercy that He allows us the privilege of forgiveness through faith in Christ. The danger in this is that there is a limit to His long-suffering, and one day, His wrath will be poured out. Thank you, Lord, that your compassion actually holds off your wrath from our lives, giving us time to ask for forgiveness. Before a person believes in the Lord Jesus Christ and repents, he stands as God's enemy. God has so much mercy for His image bearer that He sent Jesus to save us. The question that begs is, What happens to someone who rejects God's love, refuses to repent, and stubbornly clings to his sin? God will judge that person as a rebel and an enemy because God must judge sin, which also means judging the sinner. It is those who refuse the grace and mercy of God in Christ who will face eternity in hell. You can't be both His child and His enemy.

The Word of God tells us that He desires that the wicked repent of their sin and find refuge in Christ. Second Peter 3:9 NKJV states, "The Lord is not slack concerning His promise, as some count slackness, but is long-suffering toward us, not willing that any should perish but that all should come to repentance." The reason the Lord delays His second coming may be to give mankind more opportunity to repent. This also makes a prominent statement that He desires everyone saved. He doesn't desire for any to perish. Ezekiel 33:11 ASV states, "Say unto them, As I live, saith the Lord Jehovah, I have no pleasure in the death of the wicked; but that the wicked turn from his way and live: turn ye, turn ye from your evil ways; for why will ye die, O house of Israel?"

It may be difficult to understand, but God's will doesn't always come to pass when man's will is involved. He gave man the ability to choose or reject Him at the beginning of time. If one were to comply with the Lord's ways and trust in Him, then he will live. Conversely, if that same man chooses to reject the Lord, then he will die. It's not the will of God that any should perish, but the choice is ours to make. The Lord doesn't control everything, as some people teach. Yes, God is all-powerful and sovereign, but He doesn't choose to use His power in a way that denies our right to choose. Because of the choices people make, they can reject God's mercy and send themselves to hell.

Those who teach that nothing happens but what God wills are wrong. Is it His permissive will or otherwise that the unborn child should be aborted? If so, then we should not fight against that sort of evil and allow what He allows. Those who teach that God allows things to happen are only correct in the sense that God gave Adam, who was the representative of mankind, authority over this earth and over their own lives. Indeed, the Lord has absolute overall control and will bring all His promises to pass. But for now, He has withheld His judgment on the earth out of His mercy and compassion.

If the sinner repents, he is removed from the kingdom of darkness and transferred to the realm of love (see Colossians 1:13). All enmity is dissolved, all sin is removed, and all things are made new (see 2 Corinthians 5:17). This alone shows the mercy and compassion God has for the lost. It's only when we realize that sinners are the objects of His immense and holy anger that we can genuinely appreciate His mercy and compassion.

The love of God explained

No one can deny the fact that the Bible clearly teaches that God is love. First John 4:9–10 NKJV states, "In this, the love of God was manifested toward us, that God has sent His only begotten Son into the world, that we might live through Him. In this is love, not that we loved God, but that He loved us and sent His Son to be the propitiation for our sins."

Indeed, it is difficult to understand that God can flawlessly love and hate a person simultaneously. But He alone is God. He loves man as someone He created and redeem with an everlasting love and hates him for his unbelief and sinful lifestyle with the same intensity. We cannot do this as imperfect human beings because we, who believe, were once in the same predicament as the vilest sinner. We are totally unqualified to treat anyone any differently. We have no right to judge and pass sentences upon anyone, for we are no more deserving than they. Thus, we must remind ourselves to treat everybody with love and kindness. If God loves us in our imperfections, then so should we love others. This is in no way condoning a sinful lifestyle, but we pity those without Christ.

We must hate sin by recognizing it for what it is, refusing to take part in it and condemning it because it is contrary to God's nature. Sin is to be hated just as the Lord hates it, not excused or taken lightly. We love those not yet saved by showing them respect, praying for them, and witnessing the Gospel of Christ (see 1 Peter 2:17; 1 Timothy 2:1). True love will treat someone with respect and kindness even though you do not approve of their lifestyle or sinful choices. After all, God did not approve or our sinful lifestyle either.

If we genuinely love others as God loves us, we will not silently allow a person to remain in sin. If you are indeed in the love of God, then you will be compelled to warn a person of the dangerous condition they are in. They should know that sin leads to death (see James 1:15), and we are obligated to speak God's truth in love (see Ephesians 4:15). We hate sin by refusing to condone, ignore, or excuse it.

Jesus was sent here to save those who are lost. His mission was to present Himself as the Savior to whoever would believe and accept His sacrifice as payment for their sin. He didn't limit His love to just those who were willing to receive Him but for the sinner as well. Indeed, it was His great and unspeakable mercy for mankind that Christ obeyed the Father and died upon the cross. We must be clear in one point: God doesn't send sin to hell but the sinner. But praise God there is hope for those who will repent and turn to Him for forgiveness.

FOR FURTHER STUDY
Old Testament

Leviticus 20:23 NKJV: "And you shall not walk in the statutes of the nation which I am casting out before you; for they commit all these things, and therefore I abhor them."

Leviticus 26:30 NKJV: "I will destroy your high places, cut down your incense altars, and cast your carcasses on the lifeless forms of your idols; and My soul shall abhor you."

Psalm 5:4–6 NKJV: "For You *are* not a God who takes pleasure in wickedness, Nor shall evil dwell with You. The boastful shall not stand in Your sight; You hate all workers of iniquity. You shall destroy those who speak falsehood; The LORD abhors the bloodthirsty and deceitful man."

Psalm 7:11–13 NKJV: "God *is* a just judge, And God is angry *with the wicked* every day. If he does not turn back, He will sharpen His sword; He bends His bow and makes it ready. He also prepares for Himself instruments of death; He makes His arrows into fiery shafts."

Psalm 11:5–6 NKJV: "The LORD tests the righteous, But the wicked and the one who loves violence His soul hates. Upon the wicked He will rain coals; Fire and brimstone and a burning wind *Shall be* the portion of their cup."

Psalm 106:39–40 NKJV: "Thus they were defiled by their own works, And played the harlot by their own deeds. Therefore the wrath of the LORD was kindled against His people, So that He abhorred His own inheritance."

Proverbs 10:27–28 NKJV: "The fear of the LORD prolongs days, But the years of the wicked will be shortened. The hope of the righteous *will be* gladness, But the expectation of the wicked will perish."

Proverbs 16:4–5 NKJV: "The LORD has made all for Himself, yes, even the wicked for the day of doom. Everyone proud in heart *is* an abomination to the LORD; *Though they join* forces, none will go unpunished."

Jeremiah 12:8 NKJV: "My heritage is to Me like a lion in the forest; It cries out against Me; Therefore, I have hated it."

FOR FURTHER STUDY
New Testament

John 3:16–18 NKJV: "For God so loved the world that He gave His only begotten Son, that whoever believes in Him should not perish but have everlasting life. For God did not send His Son into the world to condemn the world, but that the world through Him might be saved. He who believes in Him is not condemned; but he who does not believe is condemned already, because he has not believed in the name of the only begotten Son of God."

John 3:36 NKJV: "He who believes in the Son has everlasting life; and he who does not believe the Son shall not see life, but the wrath of God abides on him."

Romans 2:5 NKJV: "But in accordance with your hardness and your impenitent heart you are treasuring up for yourself wrath in the day of wrath and revelation of the righteous judgment of God."

Ephesians 5:6 NKJV: "Let no one deceive you with empty words, for because of these things the wrath of God comes upon the sons of disobedience."

Galatians 5:19–21 NKJV: "Now the works of the flesh are evident, which are: adultery, fornication, uncleanness, lewdness, idolatry, sorcery, hatred, contentions, jealousies, outbursts of wrath, selfish ambitions, dissensions, heresies, envy, murders, drunkenness, revelries, and the like; of which I tell you beforehand, just as I also told *you* in time past, that those who practice such things will not inherit the kingdom of God."

Colossians 3:5–6 NKJV: "Therefore put to death your members which are on the earth: fornication, uncleanness, passion, evil desire, and covetousness, which is idolatry. Because of these things the wrath of God is coming upon the sons of disobedience."

1 Thessalonians 1:9–10 NKJV: "For they themselves declare concerning us what manner of entry we had to you, and how you turned to God from idols to serve the living and true God, and to wait for His Son from heaven, whom He raised from the dead, *even* Jesus who delivers us from the wrath to come."

Revelation 15:1 NKJV: "Then I saw another sign in heaven, great and marvelous: seven angels having the seven last plagues, for in them the wrath of God is complete."

Revelation 20:15 NKJV: "And anyone not found written in the Book of Life was cast into the lake of fire."

NOTES

1   Vance Havner. *Repent or Else Revell*. P. 86, 88.

2   "The Secularization of the Church." The Christian Post. https://www.christianpost.com/news/the-secularization-of-the-church.html.

3   A. W. Pink. "Studies on Saving Faith, Part I Sign of the Times."

4   Jerry Bridges. *The Pursuit of Holiness*. Paperback. https://www.barnesandnoble.com/w/pursuit-of-holiness-jerry-bridges/1100410485.

5   C. S. Lewis. The Four Loves. p. 88. (1960).

6   https://www.renewingworshipnc.org/quotes-by-tozer/

7   http://www.jonathan-edwards.org/Sinners.pdf

8   https://gracequotes.org/author-quote/Thomas Manton/

9   Andrew Wommack. *Living Commentary*. 2 Thessalonians 2:9–11.

10   A. W. Pink. *The Attributes of God*. p. 89. "Indifference to sin is a moral blemish, and he who hates it not is a moral leper."

11   https://www.merriam-webster.com/dictionary/reveal

12   https://gracequotes.org/topic/guilt/TimothyLane

13   Arthur W. Pink. *The Attributes of God*. p. 80. (Baker Publishing Group. Kindle Edition).

14   William Plumer. Commentary for Psalm 2:11. "God is indeed on a throne of grace, but that is no less glorious and suited to inspire reverence than a throne of judgment."

15   Unknown

16   David Wells. Guilt Archives. Grace Quotes. *The Attributes of God*. Chapter 16. "Worldliness is what any particular culture does to make sin look normal and righteousness look strange."

17   https://gracequotes.org/author-quote/george-whitefield/

18   Daniel Fuller. *The Unity of the Bible*. (Zondervan, 1992). p. 312.

19   Arthur W. Pink. *The Attributes of God*. p. 80. (Baker Publishing Group. Kindle Edition).

[20] https://www.brainyquote.com/quotes/vance_havner_390051

[21] *Spiritual Authority*. TELUS. http://www3.telus.net/trbrooks/spiritualauthority.pdf

[22] https://www.goodreads.com/quotes/search?q=idol+factoriesJohn Calvin

[23] https://www.goodreads.com/quotes/search?q=idol+factoriesJohn Calvin

[24] Thomas Watson. "Eternity to the godly is a day." https://www.goodreads.com/quotes/496744-eternity-to-the-godly-is-a-day-that-has-no.

[25] "Top 25 Quotes by D. A. Carson (of 121)." A–Z Quotes. https://www.azquotes.com/author/16415-D_A_Carson 79.

[26] "A. W. Pink Quotes." ChristianQuotes.info. https://www.christianquotes.info/quotes-by-author/a-w-pink-quotes.

[27] A. W. Pink. *The Attributes of God.*

[28] Jerry Bridges. *The Pursuit of Holiness*. Paperback. https://www.barnesandnoble.com/w/pursuit-of-holiness-jerry-bridges/1100410485.

[29] https://areligiousexperiment.wordpress.com/2011/09/11/i-like-your-christ-but-i-do-not-like-your-christians-because-they-are-so-unlike-your-christ-ghandi/

[30] "Top 25 Quotes by D. A. Carson (of 121)" A–Z Quotes. https://www.azquotes.com/author/16415-D_A_Carson 79.

About the Author

Rev. Timothy E. Pace is a retired firefighter of thirty-five years who now pursues the work of God as an itinerant minister. He has ministered regionally and has traveled abroad for more than thirty years. He holds credentials with the Assembly of God and attends River of Life Church located in Brandon, Mississippi, serving under Pastor Brett Nettles. The message that he preaches is what some would consider to be an old-school, traditional Pentecostal message of grace, repentance, and holiness. His greatest desire is to help the body of Christ to mature and fulfill the Great Commission of Christ by making disciples who can then, in turn, make more disciples. He is available for supply ministry, men's ministry, revivals, and other speaking engagements as required.

CPSIA information can be obtained
at www.ICGtesting.com
Printed in the USA
LVHW090007100222
710541LV00022B/129